MW00778176

Allan Degreef

# Hotel Investments & Developments

## The assessment of the decision-making factors

LAP LAMBERT Academic Publishing

**Impressum/Imprint (nur für Deutschland/only for Germany)**
Bibliografische Information der Deutschen Nationalbibliothek: Die Deutsche
Nationalbibliothek verzeichnet diese Publikation in der Deutschen Nationalbibliografie;
detaillierte bibliografische Daten sind im Internet über http://dnb.d-nb.de abrufbar.
Alle in diesem Buch genannten Marken und Produktnamen unterliegen warenzeichen-,
marken- oder patentrechtlichem Schutz bzw. sind Warenzeichen oder eingetragene
Warenzeichen der jeweiligen Inhaber. Die Wiedergabe von Marken, Produktnamen,
Gebrauchsnamen, Handelsnamen, Warenbezeichnungen u.s.w. in diesem Werk berechtigt
auch ohne besondere Kennzeichnung nicht zu der Annahme, dass solche Namen im Sinne
der Warenzeichen- und Markenschutzgesetzgebung als frei zu betrachten wären und
daher von jedermann benutzt werden dürften.

Coverbild: www.ingimage.com

Verlag: LAP LAMBERT Academic Publishing GmbH & Co. KG
Heinrich-Böcking-Str. 6-8, 66121 Saarbrücken, Deutschland
Telefon +49 681 3720-310, Telefax +49 681 3720-3109
Email: info@lap-publishing.com

Approved by: The Netherlands, NHTV Breda University of Applied Sciences, Diss., 2011

Herstellung in Deutschland (siehe letzte Seite)
ISBN: 978-3-8484-8570-3

**Imprint (only for USA, GB)**
Bibliographic information published by the Deutsche Nationalbibliothek: The Deutsche
Nationalbibliothek lists this publication in the Deutsche Nationalbibliografie; detailed
bibliographic data are available in the Internet at http://dnb.d-nb.de.
Any brand names and product names mentioned in this book are subject to trademark,
brand or patent protection and are trademarks or registered trademarks of their respective
holders. The use of brand names, product names, common names, trade names, product
descriptions etc. even without a particular marking in this works is in no way to be
construed to mean that such names may be regarded as unrestricted in respect of
trademark and brand protection legislation and could thus be used by anyone.

Cover image: www.ingimage.com

Publisher: LAP LAMBERT Academic Publishing GmbH & Co. KG
Heinrich-Böcking-Str. 6-8, 66121 Saarbrücken, Germany
Phone +49 681 3720-310, Fax +49 681 3720-3109
Email: info@lap-publishing.com

Printed in the U.S.A.
Printed in the U.K. by (see last page)
ISBN: 978-3-8484-8570-3

# Acknowledgement

Several people have contributed greatly to the realisation of this report by sharing their time and knowledge and by providing feedback. Therefore I would like to express my gratitude and deepest appreciation by a word of thank.

First and foremost, I would like to thank Jos van der Sterren, Herman Jan Meijers and Carin Rustema for their valuable guidance and assistance during my quest for a subject and the approval of this subject matter. My gratitude is also very much directed towards supervisors Leen Fokker and Pieter Piket for their respective stake of the support and constructive assistance I received for this research.

Furthermore I would like to dedicate merits and words of thank to Geoffrey Davies, tourism consultant from Euroleisure; Marc Debroye, hotel industry expert from the online hotel investment medium TourismRoi; Douwe Cramer, lecturer at NHTV and former general manager of JW Marriott Dubai; and Christian Holthof & Carlos Lanckriet, and professors Tourism & Hotel Management from Plantijn Hogeschool Antwerpen. The contact moments with these specialists have contributed significantly to my understanding of the hotel market.

In addition, I should not forget to thank Joris Vanhove and Erik Billen who are personal friends and a graduate of Applied Economics and financial planner at Optima Financial Planning and an investment consultant at KBC Bank respectively. I would like to thank them for sharing their knowledge and expertise in the field of investments.

I truly hope that this report fulfils the readers' expectations and that the analysis has the ability to contribute to the literature about hotel investments and be of perceptible value for investment seeking destinations all around the world.

# Executive Summary

This report discusses and analyses the hotel industry's development decision-makers in order to advance knowledge of the factors they assess during hotel development planning phases. These factors and criteria have been thoroughly examined in order to gauge their relative importance in hotel development decision-making and to determine the level of manageability destinations hold to adjust and modify that factor if needed.

The generation of all factors that play a role in hotel investment decision-making compels to seek contact with those who know best: the investors and developers. In the process of examining the hotel investors and developers it is inevitable to get acquainted with their strategies if one wants to achieve a total comprehension of the market and of how things work. The maze of corporate identities involved in hotel investments and developments has been uncovered and disentangled in an attempt to create a framework for the reader.

Due to the big structural changes in the nineties in which the larger hotel chains started selling their real estate the types and numbers of hotel real estate proprietors have altered significantly. Many other factors triggered the eagerness of investors to include hotel real estate in their portfolio such as the origination of different investment vehicles and disappointing or lagging revenues from traditional asset categories. Investments in the hospitality industry are regarded as holding a significant amount of risk due to the volatility of the tourism industry; nevertheless investors are willing to bear the risks if the returns on investment are proportional.

In order to detect those developing and deciding a thorough examination of all investors, of both finances and knowhow (i.e. the hotel operators), has been carried out. In this examination the most important commercial investors have been defined and presented as hotel groups, individual investors, hotel investment companies, real estate investment companies, real estate investment trusts, private equity firms and institutional investors such as banks, insurance companies and pension funds. All former are providers of equity or debt financing and in some cases provide in both. Some of these financial investors are also involved in operating the business, such as the hotel groups and some hotel investment companies. Hotel exploitation is also in many cases outsourced to an independent hotel management company.

The description and examination of the investors has made it practicable to determine those who are deciding on where and when to develop new lodging facilities. Those developers were intended to be the providers of the factors they consider while appraising a hotel development. Furthermore it was also intended to make them the assessors of the values representing the importance of the respective factors. However these methods of information-gathering proved to be impossible the examination of the investors has revealed who are the actual hotel development decision-makers. These include mainly the hotel groups yet also the hotel and real estate investment companies and the individual developers.

A hotel development always entails of a construction of a new property or of the acquisition of an existing hotel real estate or a property that can serve for it. In the process of a hotel development the decision-takers are not the only stakeholder group. Apart from the developers, described by Isaac as the clients, there are also the funders, the professional advisors, the destination's planning authority, contractors if any and the community. However they all have a stake the research's attention is only directed to those developing and deciding.

After numerous attempts of getting into the impenetrable world of hotel investors in order to obtain the very best primary data the methods of information-gathering were compelled to be changed. All factors are therefore collected only on the basis of literature and interviews with experts but despite the adjustment the list has certainly nearly reached the point of completeness. All factors have been examined and categorised according to the subject of relevance. The categories created are based on their reference to the investor, the destination, the financial feasibility of the subject project, and to the subject property or site.

The scrutinized factors referring to the investor include portfolio diversification, regulatory influence in the destination, alignment with stakeholders, existing partnership agreements and the proximity to the home office. The factors about the destination have been subdivided in different segments handling about the tourism-related factors, economic factors, socio-political factors and legislative factors. In respective order they include lodging demand (seasonality, volatility of demand, type of demand generator, niche market availability), competitive lodging supply and the accessibility of the destination; level of economic growth, economic features and trends of the market area, demographic economics and the real estate market cycle; safety & security, and political stability; and lastly the imposed zoning codes, permit and license approval processes and tax policies. For the factors referring to the financial feasibility of the subject project there has been opted to assess the importance of the return on investment, the forecasted development and operational expenses, and the forecasted revenue. The physical suitability of the site, visibility and accessibility of the property, the availability of utilities and the outcomes of a property valuation then eventually are the factors referring to the site or property.

Notwithstanding the miscellaneous of factors and criteria they all have a common trait, being their influential power in the considerations of hotel developers. For assessing and detecting the levels of importance there was initially opted to use the analytical hierarchy process, a renowned method to allot values to factors. Despite all efforts investors proved not utterly cooperative in filling out the survey created and as such the assessments of the factors have been done by means of published case studies, feasibility studies, press releases, the interviews with experts and other secondary data. All factors have been assessed with respect to their importance for hotel development decision-making and with respect to the level of manageability of the factor by the destinations' planning authorities.

However the research results were intended to be provided by means of the calculations of the survey expirations they are nevertheless representing a reflection of the reality. The financial factors proved to be paramount in nearly all of hotel developments. The level of economic growth and the features and trends of the market area both are very important for the creation of lodging demand. And also the level of lodging supply is determinant, as it has little sense to invest in a saturated market.

All of the other factors and criteria have been assessed likewise and based on the combination with the level of manageability of the factors a few general and more specific recommendations have been moulded. The creation of new demand generators and the diversification of the economy are examples of the former and increasing transparency, managing barriers to entry and making available all required data for hotel development feasibility analyses are examples of some of the more specific advices.

# Table of contents

# 1 Introduction

The area of research of this thesis is located within the realm of the hotel industry with a particular focus on hotel developments and hotel investments. Despite having completely no affinity with these topics I have selected this area of research because of an article I read a few years ago. This article described an automated model that had the ability to detect the most ideal location in Mexico for what should become the Acapulco of the east. Intrigued by the way how a time-honored Mexican fishing port could become converted into one of the earth's greatest tourism hotspots only by assessing a variety of factors I started pondering on the question on the basis of what this all was determined. As such it is the story of Cancun that established a personal determination to advance knowledge of exactly those factors that make or break a destination's hotel investment appeal.

However academic research about investments and real estate development is ubiquitous there is only few to little research about investments in the hospitality sector, with almost even none about the types of hotel investors, their behavior and the factors they consider to identify investment opportunities. It is due to this lack of an abundance of research handling about hotel investments and developments that I have written this dissertation, aspiring to fill in the research voids as valuable as possible.

The method applied for achieving the intended was to disentangle the decisions into its constituent determining factors. In the process of doing so it immediately became clear it is indispensable to study then also those players that make these decisions. For that reason I have opted to precede the examination of the factors by introductory chapters about the actual "decision-takers". Pertaining to those decision-takers and the values of importance they allot to the decision-making factors it has been my constant aim throughout the research to uncover the answers on those short yet encapsulating interrogatives "Who?", "How?", "What?" and "How Much?".

I knew the road would be bumpy, the distance to be covered vehement and the hindrances to encounter fortuitous but the determination to reach the destination has been continuous and therefore I presume it is allowed to say the driver has made a descent trip.

I genuinely hope the thesis has the ability to enhance your knowledge of hotel investment and development decision-making factors and to be of great applicable value to your personal state of affairs.

# 2 The research

This chapter introduces the research that was conducted in a period of 7 months, from August 2010 until February 2011.

As opposed to applied research this research should be interpreted as a fundamental research, a research carried out to advance knowledge of fundamental principles, in this case about the hotel industry and about hotel developments and hotel investment/development decision-making factors. However it is intended to draw conclusions that will support development planning tourism destinations the entire research is more about advancing knowledge instead of the creation of applicable methods or advice. This chosen approach will also be reflected in the research as there is opted to not work with case studies or many real-life time references in an attempt to get to unbiased and generalised assessments that apply to all.

Upcoming paragraphs will illustrate the general context of the research such as the problem statement, the goal of the research along with research questions, the research course, the methodology and the limitations encountered. A theoretical framework has also been presented to underline the contributions of the most relevant literature.

## 2.1 The problem statement

"Investing in the hospitality sector is considered by many investors to be a high-risk use of time and capital" (Rushmore, 2002). The investor not only acquires an interest in a volatile form of real estate but also participates in the highly specialized business of operating a service-oriented going concern. A diminution of this investor prudence can be achieved through increased knowledge of what the actual thresholds are for hotel investors. Before any money is committed to the purchase of a property, prudent investors perform or commission a thorough preliminary economic market study and/or feasibility study. Thus in assessing the opportunity different analyses and considerations are made, based on various criteria. While the investors are well aware of the emphasis's they put on the different criteria, many investment seekers lack this knowledge, resulting often in investment attraction constraints leaving two sides empty-handed.

## 2.2 Research goal & questions

In an attempt to replenish the investment seeking destinations' knowledge with knowledge of investors and developers about how their hotel investment decisions are constituted the following research goal has been formulated.

*To assess weights to hotel investment decision-making factors and other criteria influencing hotel investment or development decision-making, in order to advice authorised levels of government and destination management organisations on different options how to improve their hotel investment appeal.*

A main research question has been formulated that refers to the goal mentioned above. In addition sub research questions have been formulated to serve as a course of action for achieving the main goal.

Main research question

*How can hotel investment decision-making criteria and factors be assessed according to their importance and level of alterability or manageability and how can this assessment serve as the basis for recommendations towards destinations?*

Sub research questions

*Who are the investors and entrepreneurs that decide on hotel investments and hotel developments?*
*Based upon which factors and criteria do hotel investors and developers make their decisions?*
*Which factors are considered more decisive and influential than others?*

*Which are the factors that are manageable by destinations and to what extent are they manageable?*

The previous four research questions incorporate the major subject matters of the research dealt with and are the most adequate indicator of what the reader can be expecting. That there are hurdles seriously encumbering finding tailor-made answers on the research questions will become clear in chapter 2.4.

## 2.3   Research course conceptualisation

In an attempt to conceptualise the main steps of the research in the most retrenched structure possible the following conceptual schema has been created.

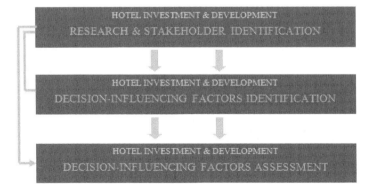

The influential factors are identified on account of the preliminary research about hotel investments and developments and the identification of the stakeholders of those processes. Relevant information about the stakeholder identification is being presented in this dissertation in an endeavour to create a framework for the reader. The identification of the factors then initiated a research on each of the respective factors in order to gain a foundation of knowledge required for the actual factor assessment. After this laborious research phase the stakeholders identified in the first research phase have been kindly asked to participate in assessing and valuing the factors, as being indicated by the arrows on the left of the scheme.

This research outline does not represent the structure of the thesis yet it indicates the importance of the stakeholders for both the factor identification as the factor assessments. When obtaining all information required via the stakeholders however proved being problematic, methods of information gathering have been slightly altered, more details hereabout in the following chapter of methodology.

## 2.4 Methodology

### 2.4.1 Bordering the coverage

The scope of an examination in which the relative weight of different hotel investment decision-making criteria is assessed is so wide that several research problems and impediments have to be taken into consideration.

With the multitude of miscellaneous stakeholders on both demand[1] and supply side[2] it is of high importance to border the research area and to clearly define all actors throughout the entire research process.

Narrowing down the scope of the research was of primordial importance to come to presentable concrete results, as there would have been even more generalised conclusions from a research that would have included even more sorts of investors and a total coverage of every potentially affecting criterion. The execution of this narrowing down has been done in assistance of an expert from a tourism destination consultancy firm.

For the investors to be covered there has been opted for focusing on commercial investors as they remain to be most heavily involved in hotel investments leading to destination growth and development (ING, 2008). However other types of investors such as governments, angel investors and NGOs are as such neglected by the research the basket of commercial investors still covers many types of investors with various methods of financing. This abundance of types of investors with their varying methods of work has been one of the major nuisances in mapping all stakeholders. Gaining full comprehension of the entire investment supply side has proved to be no effortless undertaking, yet of primordial importance to be able to detect all potential influential factors and to be able to create advice correctly. In the process of examination other important stakeholders of the hotel development have appeared to have large significance of which hotel

---

[1] i.e. Investment seeking and/or development planning destinations
[2] i.e. Commercial hotel investors and hotel developers

management companies and tourism consultancy bureaus are most relevant. However not investing financially they can evenly be defined as investors as they invest operational know-how and advice respectively.

With the exuberance of types of investors entangled further specification concerning the actual subject, the hotels, is advised. Because hotels are often classified by service type ranging from small limited service hotels to all-inclusive full-service resorts it is advised to consider the investments respectively. Variations in the weights of criteria according to the service type of the hotel are expectable as for instance it does not need research to know that visibility of the property or proximity to the demand generator is more important for a hotel catering the upscale market than one catering backpackers. Nevertheless all hotels considered for investment in this research belong to the uncomplicated classification of hotels represented in the threefold luxury, mid-market and budget-economy. This segment classification is selected since it is unsophisticated and because there anyhow is no segment classification that can claim correctness or completeness. Once more, it is not this research's aspire to specify and advise that detailed and therefore referring to segments will only occur when considered relevant and essential.

## 2.4.2 Defining the target group

As this dissertation is written in a tourism context the focus will be on how tourism destinations or tourism developing destinations can eventually respond on and gain from the conclusions of the research results. Consequently the results are not targeted to any of the described investors or hotel developers. Another specification to be made with regards to this type of target group is to decide on if the purpose of writing is directed to the public or private sector of the destination. With conclusions intended to make destinations create a more hotel investment friendly climate it is found that the public level has most of the authority due to higher level of required legislative power necessary for amending the investment climate . This decision is invigorated by the results of a study committed by the World Tourism Organisation about destination management organisations in which it is stated that almost all the DMOs support a continuing important role for the public sector in destination management and marketing. Given the fact that the private sector habitually is interwoven with or represented in the public sector, and because governments habitually defend their private sector the research's focus and recommendations are not directed to the private level of the destination. This without a total neglect, as they eventually also profit or are affected by their destination's public sector performance.

The public sector structure of a tourist destination again comprises of different levels of institutions and entities and depending on the destination it might even sometimes include a destination management organisation. Furthermore the public level incorporates different levels of authorities including those on local, municipal, regional and national levels. The power to manage the issues the criteria are based upon or the ability to influence hotel investment decision behaviour is often dispersed among the different levels of government. So for example is the stake of the municipal level on spatial planning likely higher than that of tax incentives, which is mostly regulated on a national level. However the extent of the target group covers all levels of government, it should be realised that destination management organisations also possess great influential power on decision-making within the destination, and therefore the research results might also be of value to them.

As yet informed in the previous chapter a more extensive narrowing down of the destination according to type has been considered but has not been implemented. The purpose of the research is to create a general package of hotel investment decision-making criteria weights regardless of the type of destination. The apparent reality that fluctuations occur in the importance of a criterion according to the destination type or the destinations main demand generator is taken into account but will not result in specified results. So will for example political stability might be less influential if the destination hosts a UNESCO World Heritage site than when it does only has a tropical beach similar to the one of the neighbouring and politically stable country. Or so might for example construction impediments be more influential for hotel construction in a mountainous winter resort than for a city destination. The type of destination is likely of uttermost importance for weighing the hotel investment decision-making criteria but concerning this issue the research's attempt is to create a general outcome projectable on any type of destination, whether it is a metropolis attracting hotel investments for catering the needs of the growing amount of business travellers, or for a beach side destination in a developing country eager to grow and try to enjoy the potential benefits of tourism. The latter example steers seemingly to the consideration of approaching a destination as being located in a developed or developing country. Again results in assessing weight to the different criteria can be expected to vary according to the level of development of the destination, nevertheless there is opted to obtain a generalised conclusion relevant for any tourism destination worldwide, developed or developing. The motivation for this approach is the basic assumption that the importance of for example criteria such as the availability of utilities or the return on investment remain almost entirely unchanged, regardless of being a hotel development in a developed or in a developing country. The allotment of the level of development of a country is even anyhow a contemptuous issue on itself and as such this type of bifurcation of destinations is considered not appropriate for usage in this research.

## 2.4.3    Gaining & obtaining knowledge

After outlining the investment supply and demand side another hurdle was the need for full comprehension about investment types. Intricately related with the type of investor the types of investments possess enough complicacy to create confusion among uninitiated ones, therefore it was considered essential to gain qualitative information from experts in the field of investments. Funnelling the required information and finding the correct literature about real estate investments and hotel investments not only appeared to be strenuous but also insufficient to achieve a total understanding. Without basic understandings about investments in general it is considered to be inapt to investigate the world of hotel investments. Acquiring this knowledge was considered to be achieved best through extensive reading, followed by a careful selection of relevant material. Knowledge gaps are chosen to be filled in by financial experts with sound investment knowledge from the financial banking industry.

After determination of the scope and the study of the investment supply side the criteria needed to be selected. Literature and available feasibility studies for hotel development have contributed most in this regard and were enforced by knowledge of hotel experts from universities and the tourism investment platform TourismRoi.[3]

After selection the data list was amended and improved where needed by a tourism destination consultant and transformed into a survey. A sample was created with all those involved in hotel investment decision-making, not only those who invest financial resources but also those who invest in expertise and knowledge and as such also have a significant stake in determining hotel developments. After initial research it became clear that investors often make use of the services of tourism consultant companies, therefore these advisory bodies were not excluded from the sample. Contact details have been collected by use of the internet and through relational connections. The sample, existing out of sixty-four multinational and smaller hotel investment and development decision-makers with a well considered representation

---

[3]TourismRoi: an online medium by which hotel investors and destinations can enjoy the services of massive collaboration.

based on investor type and a correct representation from every corner of the world, has been contacted by means of telephone and has been kindly invited to participate in the survey. Unfortunately, due to some limitations (see chapter 2.5), the response rate was less than five percent and therefore this method of information-gathering needed to be reconsidered. The idea to assess numerical weights to the various factors with the already examined analytical hierarchy process (AHP) was bound to fail and despite all efforts made the decision to continue the research by means of other research techniques was destined to be the sole solution.

The interviews with the experts, press releases and online hotel development case studies have together with the little seized information from the surveys been the input sources for the assessments. As methods of information-gathering about hotel investment and development decision-making these appeared to be the only available sources of all attempts. Despite being compelled to obtain the information by the use of these sources they have served as befitting by delivering what was sought for.

## 2.5    Limitations

In the process of research several limitations have to be taken into consideration by the readers of this report. Maybe partly due to the author's naivety the analysis of the factors could not ensue as it was planned. Despite all efforts it proved to be impossible to collect data and find a willingness of hotel investors and developers to participate in the disseminated survey. The reticence to reveal internal strategies is comprehensible, however I initially thought the reluctance would be less.

Another limitation encountered was the unavailability of experts that were both familiar with the hotel industry as with investments and real estate investments. I have always met people that held expertise or were acquainted with one of both so it was intricate to combine both forms of input in a whole that makes sense.

The international and multinational character of the hotel industry and the distant locations of the home offices where hotel development decisions are made equally constrained the convenience of achieving the research goal.

## 2.6   Theoretical framework

In this section the related literature has been reviewed. It is not the intention to give a detailed survey yet rather to discuss the related topics and provide a theoretical basis for the analysis. Due to the extensiveness and variety of related topics, such as for instance real estate investments, types of investments, hotel performance indicators, opportunity identification, investment climate enhancement, etcetera, it is allowed to say that the theoretical basis includes a large amount of topics. The literature about hotel investment criteria in particular however possesses much space for addendum and therefore the research only had a limited amount of material to be administered by. Nevertheless, persistence has led to a substantial amount of interesting existing literature which in the end turned out to be of far-reaching importance for this research.

As a theoretical framework, real estate investment literature proved to be most relevant and closest to the research area. Indirectly it provided directional advice about proceeding in this research process as appropriate and productive as possible. The book Property Development Appraisal and Finance by David Isaac from 1996 confirmed the necessity to realise the tremendous amount of variables concerning real estate investments. "At its simplest the financial arrangement may deal with an individual purchasing a single property with a single loan, but it is rarely this basic. Finance is generally raised by corporate entities such as property companies, using existing property and other assets as collateral for the purchase of a portfolio of assets which may include property assets, but perhaps not exclusively" (Isaac, 1996). The latter sentence, and specifically the emphasis on the common use of collateral as financing mechanism, does ignore all other contemporary ways of investing but it connects easily with the author telling that the investment market for property cannot be seen in isolation from other investment markets. For investors, investing in real estate is often a way of diversifying portfolios and is surely not less important than investing in the other two major areas of traditional investments: fixed interest securities and company stocks and shares. Apart from offering insight in the structure of the investment market, the chapter about financing property development has been of mentionable value when it comes to clearing the maze of types of real estate developers, investors and the methods of finance.

Despite similarities with the other real estate property sectors, the hotel sector needs to be considered as having other specific investment characteristics. It is a property sector closely linked to economic conditions and external events and possesses a higher volatility than the other property sectors. Other differences include the lower risk-adjusted returns, low institutional investor support, specialised industry-specific features and a performance that resembles more a business than a property (Hess et Al., 2001; Quan et Al., 2002). These unparalleled features of the hotel sector compared to other property sectors raised the awareness not to rely solely or too intensively on real estate literature. It is mainly the duality of a hotel as being a real estate property housing an operating business affected by economic conditions and many potential external events that creates the apparent need for discerning hotel investments with other property investments. Regardless the contribution of real estate investment and real estate market analysis literature more specified theories and material were sought and found in the literature of hospitality.

From a theoretical viewpoint the handbook of Rushmore (2002) has proven to be a work that provides great insight in the hospitality consultancy sector and it suggests a lot of important factors and criteria for hotel investment decision-making. The book is known as being the most used and venerable book by hotel investors and developers worldwide. In a sequential order he

17

describes all steps needed to be undertaken for making the right hotel investment or development decisions and it includes a complete understanding of the US and other international hotel industries, procedures for determining the economic feasibility of investments, criteria for choosing a management company and the fundamentals of developing, acquiring and financing a lodging facility. A very useful feature of the work of Rushmore for this research is the deductibility of investment decision-making criteria out of the informative investor guidelines. A clear look on emphasises already reveals where importance is likely awarded to a certain factor or criterion, however it does not make clear to what extent one factor is more important than the other.

The article of Newel et Al., published in the Journal of Property Investment and Finance in 2006, describes a survey committed in Australia to assess the importance of financial, location, economic, diversification and relationship factors in influencing hotel investment decision-making. This article has been the initial inspiration for perpetrating this research, chiefly because of the methods used and the easily adoptable factors described. All factors were subdivided in 25 sub-factors which during the study have been correlated a weight of importance in the process of hotel investment decision-making by Australian investors and developers. Despite the usability it was seen that although the factors are elaborately subdivided in highly relevant sub-factors, some factors are being overlooked. However this incompleteness most factors were worthwhile taking into consideration for the development of this research that attempts to reach a wider scope. The factors mused relevant were converted into the criteria a destination will have to fulfil to attract hotel investments or to create an investment friendly climate. Extrapolation of the research results to a conclusion that covers all hotel investments worldwide is not advised due to the national character of the research. Nevertheless, the research results are expected to be in the vicinity of those of the described research.

The presentation and description of these primary sources in a separate chapter is done in order to emphasise the enormous contributions of these sources of information to the research. Furthermore it was seen that there was an inability to clearly accentuate these significances only by referring to it in the analysis. All other literature and those theories that were considered not imperative to this extent are being referred to as habitual in the text. However much of the literature appears maybe outdated the quest and subsequent selection have been thorough and highly purposeful. Besides, one must make shift with what one has.

# 3 Lodging facility analysis

## 3.1 The interdependent character of a lodging facility

Whether it is a low budget hostel catering backpackers, a tropical beach side resort on a lush Caribbean island or even the Burj-el-Arab in Dubai, all lodging facilities possess two common traits; they all consist of a real estate and a hotel management. In case of a lodging facility in operation both constituent parts are unequivocally interdependent, a hotel simply requires both a property as an operational management. The comprehension of this easy-to-understand combination is of uttermost importance to be able to understand all stakeholders of the hotel industry. Whilst in some cases the real estate and hotel management belong to the same corporation or corporative body, it occurs that, when operating a hotel does not belong to the owners' core competencies, operational management is outsourced.

In the following chapters both hotel features have been described in brief and a clarification and classification of all stakeholders and their interrelations are being examined and presented.

## 3.2 Historical outline

"Along with the evolution of lodging products and the identification and pursuit of specific segments of the lodging market, the ownership and management of lodging facilities have undergone many changes" (Rushmore,

2002). Not only the partition of hotel ownership and hotel management is a change that the hotel industry has undergone, also the parties concerned and the structures of ownership have grown in number.

"Hotels have been bought, operated and traded for many years, traditionally by individuals (often families, especially in Europe and Asia) or hotel operating companies" (Jones Lang Lasalle, 2010). Until the late nineties they have not been popular targets for investment by mainstream or institutional property investors (JLL, 2010). Until then, there were no mechanisms for investing in hotel real estate for those who lack specialist knowledge of the hotel industry. A number of factors however have now made hotel property more widely accepted as a worthwhile investment target by a much broader cross-section of investors (ING, 2008).

Factors that have buckled the market domination of individual hotel owners and hotel operating companies and that have triggered and allowed other investors to join the market of hotel real estate include:

- Reducing returns in the commercial property market (i.e. real estate related to business, e.g. malls, gas stations, office towers...) coinciding with a period of strong hotel performance,
- The emergence of a number of different real estate ownership vehicles,
- Pressure on hotel operating companies to grow distribution, resulting in the increase of willingness to take on leases and sell properties
  Source: ING, 2008

The latter expansion driven factor has been most causal for what can be referred to as a sort of 'liberalisation' of the hotel market as in fact it is because of these companies' decisions that the other investors had the possibility to penetrate the market. In recent years, the multinational hotel groups and hotel chains have started a strategy in which they decided to dispose of their real estate. The cause for this strategy is the expansion race going on between most of the chains to exploit most and most value-creating hotels in emerging countries and destinations. In order to win this battle they put their real estate on the market to raise the net assets and create the ability to finance the expansion. The most important example of hotel chains implementing and executing this model are Accor, Intercontinental Hotel Group, Hilton, Marriott, and Starwood Hotels & Resorts. Pressure from shareholders, the liquidation of assets, a focus on core-business (operating hotels) and the optimising of yields on net assets are other factors than the expansion strategy that explain why the hotel real estate is being disposed by these big hotel chains and put for sale (HVS, 2010).

However and as already indicated, the entire trend of shifts in hotel real estate ownership not only originated due to the expansion driven strategies of the big hotel chains but has had many other driving forces. From the investors' side there was an increased interest to invest in hotel real estate due to increased liquidity, disappointing or lagging revenues from traditional asset categories and other real estate such as retail and office, increased transparency of the hotel real estate market, high potential for revenue (in case of successful exploitation) and also because of the raise of fiscally attractive and risk-mitigating investment vehicles (ING, 2008; NCREIF index,

2010). Despite the advantages of investments in hotel real estate they are characterised as having a higher risk, caused by the volatility of the hospitality industry. Investors are prepared to accept a higher risk, provided that the return on investment rises accordingly.

Despite the structural enlargement of the total scale of investments in existing and new hotel real estate the trend of selling hotel real estate is, according to some experts, already diminishing again due to an expected return to the owner-operator model. The quote of Dempsey, managing director of Premier Inn, illuminates well the most plausible motive for this return: "I like to own assets, not management contracts". The surge of transferring hotel real estate from hotel chains to investors/funders may then have peaked already since many investors will also be actively participating on the sell side (e.g. private equity firms) the transaction volume is expected to remain stagnant (ING, 2008).

## 3.3    Types of hotel ownership-management constructions

According to Wickford nowadays there are four different types of hotel structures that can be distinguished: privately owned and operated, franchised, leased and managed.

A privately owned and operated hotel gives an owner most operational freedom yet also the biggest risk to be borne. The hotel owner is free to make all decisions on staff, operational structure and growth but lacks the benefits of a branded company. All marketing for example is at own expense. A privately owned and operator may have investors or other with financial interest in the hotel but the ownership's structure is in one person or company's name.

In accordance with the expansion strategies of hotel brands franchise operations have become common. A franchise operation is privately owned but the owner pays an up-front fee along with ongoing royalties to purchase the franchise. In doing so, the hotel will benefit from recognition of the brand name, a proven business model and (inter)national marketing; on the contrary the owner is consequently being dependent on that brand name for its business. If the brand loses popularity the owner may likely witness this. A remark of attention has to be made to accent the difference between franchise and management, as it is not obliged for hotel owners to use the relative management of the franchising brand.

Leased hotels are also privately owned, but the physical hotel actually belongs to someone else. In most cases lease contracts involve long-term leases and it is the lessor who stipulates the conditions for the contract. In case of a lease contract the tenant pays a fixed or variable amount of rent to the real estate owner and is responsible for the exploitation.

Managed hotels are hotels that have partnered with a recognized brand to take over the day-to-day operations of the business. Quite frequently this 'manager' lends its brand name as well. When committed to a management contract the operator pays a varying percentage of gross profit to the hotel owner. For this type of contract operational revenue in first instance belongs to the hotel exploiter, as opposed to the lease contract.

In the following table the owner's involvement in the various types of hotel structures can be withdrawn.

Figure 1: The owner's involvement

| Type of hotel structure | The owner's involvement | |
| --- | --- | --- |
| | Real estate proprietorship | Hotel exploitation |
| Privately owned & operated | Proprietor | For own account |
| Franchised | Proprietor | For own account yet assisted by the franchising brand |
| Leased | Given in lease | Arranged by the tenant, for own account or outsourced |
| Managed | Proprietor | Outsourced |

Source: own elaboration

In the subsequent chapters all stakeholders operating in one these types of hotel structures are described and discerned according to their interest in real estate ownership or hotel management. Ensuing the categorisation and induced knowledge of all stakeholders the level of involvement in hotel development decision-making will be more effortlessly demonstrable.

## 3.4 Hotel real estate: the investors concerned

Examination of hotel real estate proprietorship has demonstrated that there is an abundance of people or corporate entities involved in hotel real estate investments. Their identification is essential for the report in order to distinguish the decision-making developers, those legal entities that may affect tourism destinations' performances and futures reminiscently.

An extensive and time-consuming examination will in any case precede the moment that a laity can say he has a level of hotel investments knowledge that allows him to simply identify all investors concerned, therefore this chapter will give them a leg up. Research has shown that contemporary virtually all hotel real estate worldwide is in hands of individuals, hotel groups, real estate investment companies, hotel investment companies, real estate investment trusts, private equity firms or institutional investments. In order to find out their levels of importance in hotel development decision-making they are all separately examined with attention given to their involvement in hotel exploitation and representations in boards.

Due to the names that are sometimes tedious and lengthy there has been opted to sometimes refer to particular investors with abbreviations, such as HIC for hotel investment company or REIT for real estate investment trust. This measurement is taken to moderate the readers' ease of reading and inhibit the need for constructing overlong sentences.

### 3.4.1 Classification according to type of corporate entity

#### 3.4.1.1 Hotel groups

Paradoxically it are the hotel groups that are being described first in the chapter of hotel real estate stakeholders. The hotel groups are de facto management companies that hold different hotel chains that exploit a group of hotels together under a brand and business agreement. On the other hand it is evident as well. However these groups of hotel management companies are the providers of the 'brains' they have a history and present of possessing many 'bricks' too.

The ten largest hotel groups according to number of rooms are Intercontinental Hotel Group, Wyndham Hotel Group, Marriott International, Hilton Hotels, Accor Group, Choice Hotels, Best Western, Starwood Hotels & Resorts, Carlson, the Jumeirah Group and Global Hyatt. These hotel groups include most of famous hotel chains such as Holiday Inn, Crowne Plaza or Formula 1, all well-known and brands with maintained reputations (MKG Hospitality, 2010).

Hotel groups are an example of the owner-operator structure for many decades albeit that the growth of popularity of franchise agreements took off throughout the years and gradually decreased the need for the actual possession of the real estate by these proclaimed hotel management companies. While implementing the new expansion driven strategies the multinational hotel groups considered much of the hotel real estate vendible and sold the properties to other hotel real estate investors on the market. However there is a strong willingness for hotel management companies to keep their most prestigious and eminent hotels in strategic locations, increased demand of predominantly high net-worth individuals for exactly those 'trophies' raises the prices until levels that are high enough to sometimes even possess persuasiveness to sell.

The trend that is seen with large hotel chains to dispose real estate does not apply to the smaller hotel chains. Self-assurance is considered as important as growth for these smaller chains and because the real estate serves as collateral and as such enhances the capability to lend their properties are being kept (ING, 2008). In recent times also the larger chains started reconsidering their strategies of selling the real estate (Dempsey, 2010).

### 3.4.1.2    Individual proprietorship

In describing individual hotel proprietorship one should make distinction between the three possibilities to own a hotel as an individual. One could be:

- an owner-operator,
- an individual investor,
- or a single-tenant.

The formation of a hotel in which the individual owns and operates the hotel is the most conventional hotel structure and this type of hotel ownership goes as far as the history of the hospitality industry. Even more, it has soared and dominated the industry until the late nineties (ING,2008) and up until the moment of writing, this type of hotel ownership structure is, with varying levels per continent, a widely used type of hotel ownership. They mostly consist of family-run businesses or private-company-run businesses of which the individual is then the corporate body.

Individual investors who lack specialist knowledge and operational know-how have also obtained the possibility to include hotel real estate in the portfolio by means of equity investing. In most cases, individual investors entrust and deposit their capital to asset managers such as real estate investment banks, real estate investment companies, hotel investment companies, REITS or private equity firms. These corporate entities allow individuals to invest in hotel real estate with acceptable levels of risk. There is no involvement with hotel exploitation however depending on the share they hold they may hold representation in the board of directors.

High net-worth individuals, people with net assets surpassing 1 million US$ (ING, 2008), are also attracted to hotel real estate investments. Whereas for most investors financial gain is the driving force for putting money at risk, high net-worth investors also possess hotels for prestige. They develop prestigious hotels and resorts and have often acquisition interests for some of world's most famous and eminent hotels in strategic destinations. Because the high net-worth individuals mostly become single-tenant, they have high levels of involvement and dominant positions in the boards. Hotel management is outsourced.

### 3.4.1.3    *Real Estate Investment Companies & Hotel Investment Companies*

A relatively newly arisen group of hotel real estate owners include the real estate investment companies and the hotel investment companies. Both corporate entities have a degree of resemblance however there are some palpable differences noteworthy. They are similar as both act in a fiduciary capacity for their shareholders but there is an important difference with regard to the proprietorship of real estate that distinguishes both.

Real estate investment companies develop and finance all types of real estate including hotels and resorts, albeit the latter is not their specialisation. Therefore, as they have little to no knowledge of the hotel industry and of the operational management of a hotel they are not fanatical to keep the real estate. As soon as the project is finished, the property is being sold. They operate according to *"develop & sell"* deportment. Only in some cases, when there is no immediate buyer, they will try to find a hotel operator for a temporary management contract or lease contract.

Opposing to REICs hotel investment companies core business is hospitality-based. HICs pursue properties in key markets that offer the potential for high revenue growth in order to maximize profits and drive stockholder value. Kingdom Hotel Investments, Trinity Hotel Investors L.C.C., HEI Hotels &

Resorts, Summit Group inc., Miramar Hotel and Investment Company, MHI Hospitality Corporation and Maritz Wolff & Company are examples of some of world's largest hotel investment companies.

HICs develop hotels and resorts in order to position them and make them profitable businesses. In doing so, they are often affiliated with a franchisor and at times also with a hotel management company. These partnerships provide shareholders with peace of mind that the properties are being well-managed, which increases the likelihood and scale of beneficial returns on investment for investors.

*3.4.1.4    Real Estate Investment Trusts*

Corporate entities investing in real estate, such as the previously described REICs and HICs, are sometimes attributed a tax designation which alters their statute into a Real Estate Investment Trust (REIT). The REIT structure is designed to provide a similar construction for investments in real estate as a mutual fund provides for investments in stocks or shares.

The first REITs are born in the USA and date back as far as the 1960s, yet they only became popular in the 1990s, synchronously with the upcoming trends of the big chains to sell their real estate and the growth of popularity of franchise agreements. Nowadays, many countries know similar instruments, however not always similarly named. G-REITs (Germany), FBIs ( the Netherlands), Vastgoedbevaks (Belgium), SIICs (France) and FIIs (Italy) are examples of what in Anglophone countries such as Great-Britain, the USA and Australia is referred to as REITs. The differences lye for instance in amounts of percentages of due remittances of operational revenue and the percentages of allowed 'free float', the amount of saleable shares (WDP, 2010).

The attributed tax designation reduces significantly or eliminates entirely the corporate income taxes of the real estate investors, hence REITs can offer investors high yields and a highly liquid method of investing in real estate. Both sides are benefited. In order to gain more profitable success REITs often have specializations, such as retail, office, industrial, residential and hospitality. For the latter, the HICs are the most specialized examples; however other corporate entities, both public as private, can also be a REIT investing in hospitality real estate. REITs can be classified as equity, mortgage, or hybrid.[4]

### 3.4.1.5    Private equity firms

"A private equity firm is an investment company that pools investor funds that are utilized, generally in combination with large amounts of borrowed capital, for the acquisition of underperforming businesses. Private equity firms often choose to replace management, revamp operations, and recapitalize the balance sheet in an effort to improve profitability and increase the value of the acquired business before offering it for sale" (The

---

[4] Equity = holding shares, mortgage = debt financing, hybrid = combination

American Heritage Dictionary of Business Terms). In the hospitality industry, however, mergers are regular as well since a private equity firm often cooperates with the hotel group or hotel management company the real estate was already used by.

Due to the same trends that have positioned other hotel investor's the private equity firms have also gained a more prominent position in the hotel real estate market and according to ING private equity will continue to remain very important for the market. Some of the largest hotel real estate owning private equity firms are Blackstone Group, Whitehall (Golden Sachs), and Lehman Brothers Real Estate Partners (respective websites, 2010)

As their key business is to revitalize underperforming enterprises these companies focus on *"buy, restructure & sell"* rather than *"buy & hold"* (ING, 2010). These strategies keep transactions in hotel assets remain high and as a result the market is holding its liquidity. Despite the short investment horizon of most private equity firms they own a significant share of hotel real estate.

### 3.4.1.6    Banks, Pension Funds & Insurance companies

Institutional investors such as banks, pension funds and insurance companies have also claimed a share of the hotel real estate market since the structural shift of hotel real estate. Despite the collective term 'institutional investors' the constituents' methods of investing vary. Pension funds' and

33

insurance companies' asset managers invest indirectly through investment in other hotel investment companies or structures such as REITs, HICs or private equity firms. Banks, in contrary, also occasionally provide venture capital or debt capital directly to borrowers after feasibility plan and business plan study and approval.

Another important actor that belongs to the generically named group of institutional investors is the group of real estate investment banks and investment banks investing in real estate. These two groups are providers of capital raising and advisory services for clients in the real estate industry. Renowned REIBs and investment banks include John B. Levy & Co, Merrill Lynch, Greenhill & Co, Keybank, and Keefe, Bruyette and Woods. The investment banks' job content is two-fold; financial consultancy and provider of access to the capital markets. As for the advisory work, they give financial advice for real estate ventures and acquisitions, inclusively for hotels and other lodging facilities. Furthermore, because of their array of professional relationships they can often offer access to capital from a wide range of sources. The combination of expertise and capital availability makes them proficient capital raisers for project developers and hotel owners.

## 3.4.2 Classification according to Greer & Kolbe

The classification proposed by Greer & Kolbe in which real estate investors are categorised according to the nature of their claims and their level of operations suites perfectly as a reference for hotel investor classification.

Firstly, distinction is made between active and passive investors. "An active investor acquires direct title to real estate in which they invest, and either oversee its operation themselves or hire professional property management firms to handle day-to-day supervisory chores" (Greer et al., 2003). Their key distinguishing characteristic is that they make decisions that directly affect operating results, most often by an approbation of a professional management company or by carrying out the exploitation personally. All strategies and operational tasks of managing the hotel (e.g.: selection of on-site personnel, negotiation of maintenance contracts and any other decision-making authority...) are being discussed and determined by these active investors.

In contrary, passive investors make no operating decisions. "Passive investors turn their wealth over to professional asset managers, who in turn acquire interests in real estate, or they acquire shares in corporations, partnerships, or trusts that hold extensive real property interests" (Greer & Kolbe, 2003). Passive investors have little to no affiliation with the lodging facility they invest in. Their investment is purely financial and comprises even no investment of knowledge or expertise. Passive investors are mostly represented in the board of directors and as such also have a significant stake; nonetheless their involvement in the actual exploitation of the lodging facility is negligible.

The other way of categorizing is based on the nature of the investment. For this categorization distinction is made between investment in real assets, being sites and properties, and investment in real-estate related assets such as mortgage-backed promissory notes (Greer et al., 2003). For investment in real assets the investor literally buys interests in real property and is referred to as equity investing. Equity investors invest money in return for a percentage of the total shares and a percentage of the profits. This percentage of the monthly cash flow makes equity investors more expensive yet more abundantly available due to increased potential for higher returns. Usually though much of the purchase money comes from a mortgage lender: a debt investor. A debt investor invests money in a project for a fixed rate of return. An actual loan on the underlying property is made and there is an agreement about the payment of a certain interest rate. Monthly payments over a certain amount of time are made until the loan is paid in full. However the distinction many of the hotels are financed by a combination of equity and debt.

In the following table the range of commercial hotel investors, discerned by type of corporate entity, have been allocated to a combination of previously described options to categorize.

Figure 2: Classification according to Greer & Kolbe

| | Debt investing | Equity investing |
|---|---|---|
| Active investing | | Hotel investment companies |
| | | Hotel Groups |
| | | Individual investors |
| | | Real estate investment trusts |
| Passive investing | Real estate investment banks | Real estate investment companies |
| | Banking companies | Real estate investment banks |
| | Pension funds | Banking companies |
| | Insurance companies | Pension funds |
| | Real estate investment trusts | Insurance companies |
| | | Hotel investment companies |
| | | Real estate investment trusts |
| | | Private equity firms |

## 3.4.3 Hotel real estate capital flows

Despite the exuberance of hotel real estate investors there is only a portion of the amalgam that needs most attention with respect to the research; namely the active investors as categorized in figure 2.

The hotel groups, the HICs & REICs (REITs) and the individual owner-operators are the investors accountable for the realization of a decent management of the subject property(-ies) and as such for the success of the lodging facility. It is within these parties concerned that the developers are employed and it is them who are sought for.

The relation between the passive investors and the active investors, as categorized according to Greer & Kolb, can be easily depicted by means of a scheme that represents the most important capital flows between all hotel real estate investors.

Figure 3: hotel investment capital flows

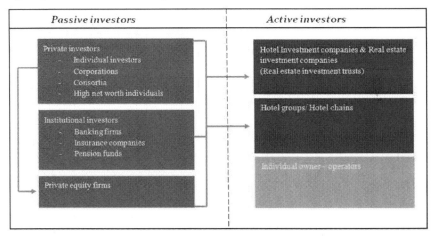

This figure clearly illustrates the major flows of financial assets from the finance providers to those stakeholders having involvement in exploiting the lodging facilities or in arranging this exploitation by for instance outsourcing it. This figure is not all-embracing and does not represent transaction volumes but anyhow facilitates the understanding of the capital flows for those not acquainted with the subject matter.

Despite the passive investors' lesser involvement in hotel operation and management their injection of capital generally confers entitlement to be represented in the Board of Directors or the Board of Managers. Thus in hotels where the structures are accordingly the passive investors do have a role in which they –jointly with the other members of the boards- execute a monitoring role on hotel management by overseeing the hotels' activities. As a consequence these investors are in cases authoritative when deciding for most appropriate hotel management. The three existing sorts of liable hotel exploiters are being outlined in the following chapter.


## 3.5   Hotel exploitation: the operators concerned


However investments are mostly perceived as being injections of financial capital, one could also consider the contribution of knowledge and know-how to be an investment. The parties handing over these assets are therefore not insignificant and are in most cases already consulted during the hotel development planning phases (Rushmore, 2002).


"The value of hotel real estate is utterly dependent on the exploitation of the hotel" (ING 2010), for this reason hotel operators are in most cases involved in hotel investment decision-making. In some cases the hotel operator is also the owner of the real estate, such as in the private owner-operator structure or in those hotels both owned and operated by hotel groups. The actual exploitation however is frequently outsourced, mainly when it is no principal dexterity or does not belong to the core competencies of the owner, such as with HICs or REICs.

The set of stakeholders of the hotel management or hotel operation component is significantly smaller and consequently less difficult to fully grasp than the stakeholders that own the hotels' real estate. As depicted in the figure, there are three types of hotel operators: private operators, hotel chains and hotel management companies.

Figure 4: The hotel exploiters

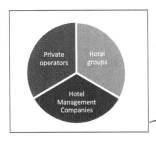

Operating and managing hotels are the hotel groups' core business activities, therefore in many cases hotel groups are also referred to as hotel management companies. The principal difference is that hotel groups are often both owner and operator while the HMCs are only operator. So as previously indicated, apart from being proprietors of hotel real estate the hotel groups mainly operate and manage hotels, not necessarily carrying one of their brands. Peculiarly, a hotel group might as such manage a hotel that is owned or franchised by one of its competitors.

The management of a hotel can also be outsourced to a hotel management company. Examples of some of the industry's most renowned hotel management companies are HVS Hotel Management, Interstate Hotels & Resorts, Winegardner & Hammonds Inc. and LTD Management Company. The hotel management companies endeavour to produce measurable results in revenue performance, guest satisfaction, cost management and profitability in a continuous attempt to improve profit margins for the hotel

40

owners. The hotel management companies are the hotel owners' partners that possess the resources, adroitness and experience to effectively operate hotels.

In the regularly smaller privately owned and operated hotels the day-to-day operational management is in hands of the person or company that owns the real estate. The deficiency of outsourced hotel management does not signify an inferior level of professionalism, albeit that in many privately owned and operated hotels imperfections and shortcomings in service are more common, especially in hotels that cater the lower segments. Justified by own experience these so-called lower levels of service can be detected more in developed or developing market areas.

To conclude one can declare that due to the influence of the exploitation on the value of the real estate those agreed on managing the subject hotel are for the most part involved in the hotel investment decisions taken.

# 4 The Hotel development

## 4.1 Introduction

After the gain of full comprehension of the hotel industry with its constituent investors the research pursues with the selection of investors involved in the development process. These investors are considered most relevant to the research as they are the decision-makers to whether or not to undertake the hotel development in that particular destination. The examination of the stakeholders of both hotel components has significantly facilitated indicating the parties concerned in hotel development decision-making.

Despite the decisive power of the previously described investors they are not the only stakeholders of a hotel development. In order to create a framework in which they operate all development parties' involvement is briefly elucidated, preceded by a chapter intended to define the two types of hotel developments. Appendix 1 provides the reader with supplementary information about the phases in the hotel development time line.

## 4.2 Hotel development types

A hotel development always entails or the development of a new property or the acquisition of an existing facility (Rushmore, 2002). This breakdown is important in regard to the hotel decision-making factors to be discussed in the following chapters.

The development of a new property may involve the construction of an entirely new real estate or it may concern a conversion from a not hospitability-related property into a lodging facility.

The acquisition of an existing facility on the other hand refers to the take-over of a hotel or resort for sale. The acquisition of an existing facility nevertheless also often includes some drastic changes with regard to both the property and the management, as possibilities exist that the hotel will cater a totally different market segment or niche market. In that sense, the acquisitions of existing facilities are not only being regarded as the contributors to the hotel investments transaction volume but also as a type of hotel development.

During the planning and implementation stages of a development that involves a construction there are factors to assess the feasibility of the project that are different than those of a hotel development in the form of an acquisition of an existing hotel. Therefore the factors influencing hotel development decision-making will be clearly allotted to one of the two types of hotel developments when applying to one development specific only.

Both types of hotel developments require proper planning and are therefore initiated by a tremendous amount of preliminary studies of which the project

43

feasibility study and the economic market study are the two most important ones. Rushmore has outlined all steps of both the planning as the implementation stage of both types of hotel developments in which in sequential order these studies are coming across, but since it has no immediate contribution to the research this matter is not discussed and presented. The stages and accompanying literature however have been analysed and disentangled in order to detect the influencing factors.

Ahead of advancing to the chapter in which the factors are being described the hotel development process has to be contextualised by indicating the stakeholders. Without the classification of the stakeholders it is not clearly visible who has which role and who are the other players not to be neglected. Moreover it proved valuable for the formation of the sample of interviewees.

## 4.3  Hotel development: the stakeholders concerned

The process of a hotel development knows many stakeholders of whom some occasionally have differing interests. Nevertheless, most of the stakeholders work in a cooperative manner to achieve what is intended to be beneficial for many; the development of a new lodging facility. In respect to the research goal further elaboration will be more extensive on those stakeholders that have the biggest stake in the actual decision where, when and what type of hotel to develop. For the completeness of the research, however, all stakeholders have been mentioned and described at least in brief.

The classification of the parties in real estate development processes of Isaac (2010) has been considered best extrapolative to serve for classifying the stakeholders regarding hotel developments. According to Isaac's finding the six main parties involved in the development process are the clients, the professional advisers, the planning authority, the funders, the contractor, and the community.

## 4.3.1 The clients

The clients, buying the opportunity, or more tangibly buying the site or property if becoming proprietor, are considered one of the most important stakeholders with respect to this research. What is defined by Isaac as the clients will be further referred to as the project developers and has to be considered as such. Their importance for this research is derived from their responsibility in terms of actual lodging facility development decision-making. A destination is fully obsequious to the hotel developers since their tourism growth is submissive to their decision-making. It needs to be emphasised that in case of promising investment opportunities on offer a destination will not have to dread not to be able to attract these hotel developers, however still the opportunity is constructed out of many variable factors that can alter the opportunity significantly and sometimes abruptly. The hotel developers and developing owners are those accountable for assessing these factors and in some cases they are assisted by consultancy firms (see chapter 4.3.3). When according to the project evaluations and feasibility studies the project is considered viable it is they who will give the fiat to the project and seek investments when needed.

The examination of lodging facilities as outlined in chapter 3 was essential to detect the players involved in hotel development and hotel industry experts' confirmations avowed the project developers to include the hotel groups, REICs, HICs and individual developers.

Despite the categorisation there is still a high degree of complicacy and interconnectedness within this selected category of stakeholders. This is due to the dual character of the hotels as previously described. For instance in case of a franchise or in case affiliated management partners the REICs, HICs and private developers will work in a cooperative manner with suppliers of these services such as the hotel chains or hotel management companies. As a result these parties are also often involved in the decision-making processes because for the benefit of the project these partnerships are likely and as such mostly made as early as possible in the development process (Rushmore, 2002).

As a summary to this subchapter it can be said that a hotel development decision is always made in agreement with multiple hotel industry players when not operating in a 'privately owned-privately managed'-structure without a franchising brand. For all other structures hotel development decisions are mostly made in unanimous agreements between two or more corporate entities providing or ideas, management, a brand, and in many cases also the funds.

## 4.3.2 The funders

In case the hotel development is not funded by the developer and funds are required, the funders also have a noteworthy stake in the success of a project. Distinction has to be made however between the providers of short-term funds for the development and the providers of long-term funds in the event of a buyout or partnership arrangement at the end of the development.

In this chapter, the funders refer to the capital providers for the development of a hotel. The providers of the short-term funds for the development, however, are in many cases also the actual future owners and as such long-term funds providers, yet this is not always the case. Many developers develop a hotel in order to sell it after project completion. Developers operating according to this 'develop & sell' approach are the REICs and some individual developers.

In contrast the hotel groups, hotel investment companies and private or individual investors developing hotels are in many cases also funder of the project, however co-funding is still often required and obtained with institutional investors such as institutional banks, insurance companies or pension funds. An elaboration on the different types of funders of hotel investments has previously been presented in chapter 3.4.1.

### 4.3.3 The professional advisors

Other indispensable members of the hotel development process include the professional advisors. The architect, the quantity surveyor[5], the planning consultant and possibly a consulting engineer, construction manager or a project manager can all have a significant consulting role in the process of hotel development. For this research the planning consultant, or tourism consultant, is most important as it is they who often commit the project evaluations and feasibility studies and consult to the hotel developers and investors whether a proposed project is economically interesting. Their advice and expertise is therefore often of immense importance in the decision-making process.

### 4.3.4 The planning authority  *Zoning/Planning etc*

The planning authority of the destination is responsible for all the matters concerning hotel developments. Actual executive authority is usually vested in a local authority whose staff is charged with implementing investment supports under guidelines issued by elected officials (Baum & Mudambi, 1995). While in some cases the authority lies with the municipal level of government, depending on the matter to be dealt with the level of authorities can vary. The planning authority is also in charge for amending policies to encourage hotel developments. The authority is theirs, however it

---

[5] A quantity surveyor estimates the costs of a new building construction or a renovation

will be seen that many characteristics of the market area are difficult to alter in an instance.

Hotel development decision-making can also be carried out by the planning authority but the need for capital makes the destination in most cases dependant on the external funding. Therefore it is not the planning authority but the funders that hold the most powerful position when it comes to hotel developments, and as such, due to the prerequisite character of accommodation, also for the destination's tourism growth.

## 4.3.5 The contractor

However according to Isaac the contractor refers to the building contractor it has been proposed that for outlining the most important stakeholders of hotel developments it applies more to the contractors of management contracts or franchise contracts. While the contracted franchising brands have less influence during the development phase of a hotel the companies exploiting the facility often do, however depending on the initiative of the developer.

## 4.3.6 The community

The community residing in the neighbourhood of the hotel development is another stakeholder not to be neglected. Local residents may have views on the proposed development that do not concur with the investor's development proposal or the planning authority's development intentions. Pressure groups and specific interest groups can therefore impede or hamper a hotel development significantly.

## 4.4 Conclusion

After examination of all hotel investors and developers with the environment they operate in one can effortlessly summarise who are the parties concerned to be taken into account by destinations' planning authorities. Regardless of their involvement in hotel management the parties involved most heavily and decisively in hotel development decision-making can be listed as follows: the hotel groups, the HICs, the REICs and the individual developers. Tourism consultants are also important decision-makers, as they are often consulted by the developers for assessing their projects' feasibilities. All these types of corporate entities have been included in the sample and have been invited to participate in the research by indicating and assessing the factors considered in their decision-making processes.

# 5   Hotel investment decision-making criteria

## 5.1   Introduction

In this chapter the rationale for the various hotel investment decision criteria is presented. It concerns a motivation for the selection by an elucidation on every single criterion. As the criteria often can be described as broad terms and concepts which are often an area of study by themselves, elaboration will not be profound. The following subchapters will serve as support for decent comprehension of the relevance of these criteria for this research; they are no attempt to amplify on and criticise every body of knowledge existing about these factors or criteria.

With a myriad of factors eventually having the potential to influence hotel investment decision-making, selection is advised.   Incorporation of for instance emotional factors affecting the investment decision-making is also considerable but keeping the research goal in mind it is of lesser importance. All factors need also to possess a degree of manageability by the destination, even if they take time or seem unfeasible.   One could argue that it is also possible to affect investors emotionally but these methods are no exact science while all other criteria are easy measureable or definable.

It should be indicated that not all of the following factors apply to all of the propounded investors and developers, for example due to investor-related strategies, nevertheless there has deliberately been opted to describe them in an uncomplicated consecutive order. To illustrate the former, a project developer handling according to a 'construct & sell' strategy will likely be less worried about the operational expenses during the financial feasibility of the project than about the development costs. As such, not all factors do always apply to all developers or investors.

Furthermore it may appear that some identified factors seem to be irrelevant and others paramount in hotel development or investment decision-making. These assumptions may of course hold verity but it is the research's attempt to verify the assumptions by assessing them.

The two terms investment and development are most often very similar in meaning, even though an investor not necessarily takes part in the development of a hotel. This is the case when an investor buys the property or equity of the property after development completion. These types of investors have also been referred to in the dissertation as funders but to avoid a complication that is semantic only, the two terms investor and developer are being used interchangeably.

## 5.2  Categorising the factors

Literature written by hotel investment experts, and chiefly the article of Newell et Al., has indirectly provided many of the factors. What can be referred to as a list of factors has then been approved and completed by a tourism consultant. After completion an obvious sequence is to classify and herewith different approaches were possible. As the list with factors at first appeared to be an amalgam of highly dispersed types of factors, a reference was needed to base the classification upon.

Since some factors refer to the destination, whether national, regional or municipal, and some to the proposed property or site, this would have been a way to classify if there was no neglect of some factors not referring to one of both. Another consideration was to classify according to whether the hotel development consists of a new construction or a property acquisition. This would however have led to an overlap of factors relevant for both, resulting eventually in an extended survey completion time which is also not favourable. In anticipation on the analysis of the research results it became evident that classification really was essential, it was furthermore realised that the decision how to classify must be made on the basis of the calculations of the research results, initially thought to be done by the AHP method. Six factors, based partly on those of Newell et al., have therefore been created, consisting out of different sub-factors. These factors are shortly described as financial, economic, diversification, destination, site and property and relationship and are created based on their reference.

After the unsuccessful attempt to obtain quantitative data from hotel investors and developers through the use of surveys the relevance of the six chapters has been reconsidered. The compelled decision to obtain data through other means of information-gathering has nullified the need for a profound disentanglement of factors and allowed grouping the factors according to their liaison in the hotel development process. The criteria and factors are therefore classified according to their reference to the investor, the destination, the real estate and the project's financial feasibility.

## 5.3 Investors' and developers' strategic factors

A destination may offer various hotel investment opportunities but if it fails to attract the attention of hotel investors the opportunities vanish and the tourism growth is halted. While it can be considered that investment opportunities hardly remain unnoticed it is of great value for destinations to have an understanding of some factors intricately related to those actors deciding.

Figure 5: general portfolio diversification

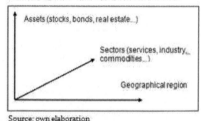

Source: own elaboration

For investors, a commonly used technique to reduce risk is investing in a variety of assets, a strategy also referred to as **portfolio diversification**. "If the asset values do not move up and down in perfect synchrony, a diversified portfolio will have less risk than the weighted average risk of its constituent assets, often less risk than the least risky of its constituents" (Sullivan, 2003). Any risk-averse investor will therefore diversify to at least some extent, including real estate and hotel investors. Mitigating risk by diversifying the portfolio can be done by investing in different types of assets, in different sectors or by spreading geographically (figure 5).

Figure 6: real estate portfolio diversification

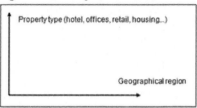

Source: own elaboration

55

For real estate investors however, it is stated by Eichholtz et al. that the conventional approach to defining diversification categories is to use property type and geographical region (figure 6). A diversified real estate portfolio can for instance include hotel assets together with other types of property such as offices, shop or retail, and this in different cities, regions or countries. When solely investing in the hospitality industry, as for example hotel investment companies and hotel groups, a diversified portfolio will include assets that are diversified according to brand or segment, respectively referred to as brand diversification or segment diversification (figure 7). The other conventional approach in real estate portfolio construction is diversifying geographically. Due to differential performances of countries and regions a well mused dissemination of investments geographically can also significantly reduce investors' risk. Despite some associated problems, the combination of property type and geographical region classifications is considered as the most adequate tool for investors to construct portfolios (ING, 2008).

Figure 7: hotel investment portfolio diversification

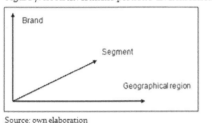

Source: own elaboration

For developers, the decision to invest in a particular destination is not based solely on the prospected return on investments but can for instance also be influenced by relational factors. When the developer possesses a degree of **regulatory influence** in the subject destination or when the developer is well **aligned with stakeholders** there is a good possibility that the hotel development decision-making is affected. Those investors who are not involved in the operation of the lodging facility, such as for instance REIBs, HICs or high net-worth individuals, can potentially also be influenced by established **partnership agreements** with management companies or franchisors. For those who are involved in the operational character of a lodging facility **proximity to the home office** has also been detected as a potential influential factor.

## 5.4 Project's financial feasibility factors

The chapter about the project's financial feasibility refers to the financial aspects concerning the hotel development. Be means of various analytical tools the experts executing the feasibility studies deliver the calculated prospects to the investor/developer. Factors such as the return on investment and projected revenue and expenses are of such decisive extent for the larger majority of the investors and developers that they are therefore included in the list of decision-making factors.

Despite the importance of the financial factors the destinations hold little power to alter the calculated estimations directly. They however hold the power to alter some of factors leading to those estimates, including the other factors described in this research. One could argue that the financial prospects are a result of the other factors and should therefore not be considered as a factor by itself; however, for many investors and developers the calculated results from a feasibility study confirm their identified opportunity as potentially lucrative and sometimes therefore they suffice as determinant.

In this chapter the financial factors are described shortly yet the technical analyses to calculate the prospects are not, due to the lesser relevance to the research. Finance, being a fund management science, deals with the interrelation of the concepts of time, risk and money and these aspects are all interwoven with and dealt with in the decision-making factors elucidated upon in the following subchapters.

As an approach for the evaluation of the financial consequences of an investment, the **forecasted Return on Investment** (ROI) serves as a commonly used mechanism for investors and for developers as an effective depicter of the economic feasibility of a project. However it is widely assumed that any investment is made with the purpose of gaining financial benefit, this is not always the case. Therefore in this research return on investment is not considered solely as presumed investment or development goal but included in this chapter in the listing of potential influential factors in the decision-making. Although it is a correct postulation that it is in almost all cases of highest importance, for investors there is a serious disadvantage with using it as the sole basis for decision-making. It is argued by many financial experts that the ROI by itself says nothing about the likelihood that expected returns and costs will appear as predicted and as such it says nothing about the risk of an investment. For diminishing that risk it is argued by many that a proper investment analysis should also measure the probabilities of different ROI outcomes. In case of an acquisition, the historical rates of return are also taken into account albeit past performance has shown to be no reliable predictor of future performance, particularly when changes have been made to hotel management or franchise affiliation or when tourism environment altering trends have been noted. For calculating the ROI, investors and investing developers can make use of various arithmetical calculations which consider many of the other described factors from this research.

However embedded in the previous factor, the **forecasted development expenses** are another important consideration in hotel investment decision-making and are handled separately because they apply only to those involved in the actual development process. The hotel development costs, being construction or acquisition and renovation costs are depicted as cost per unit. Consequently cost per room is selected as benchmark for representing the expenses involved in constructing a new hotel or acquiring and renovating an existing property. These expenses can include land acquisition costs, site preparation costs, construction or renovation costs, furniture and equipment purchasing, professional fees, development fees and transaction and loan fees (Rushmore, 2002). When development costs for a particular site or in a certain market area are in excess of the tolerable the financial feasibility can be jeopardized. It has often been proved that for the hotel industry not only literally the sky is the limit so it occurs rarely that promising projects are withdrawn, although due to for instance remoteness of the destination or the unavailability of required commodities projects can be cancelled. Regarding the mitigation of development costs; when operating under a brand or in cooperation with a hotel management company economies of scale carry the potential to decrease development expenses significantly.

Apart from development costs there are other expenses a lodging facility will incur. These expenses can be listed as **forecasted operational expenses** and categorised according to the standardised system outlined in *Uniform System of accounts for Hotels*. The categories in this system include rooms, food and beverage, administrative and general, sales and marketing, property operations and maintenance, utilities, management fees, and fixed charges such as rent, property and other taxes, and insurance. This factor applies most to those developers involved in the eventual management of the subject hotel; however it is a factor best considered by all developers. The fixed and variable approach is a commonly used method for estimating forecast expenses (Rushmore, 2002).

The aforementioned use of rooms as a unit is also applied with forecasting the revenue of the proposed hotel in operation, i.e. the **forecasted operational revenue**. Revpar, short for revenue per available room, is a ratio commonly used to measure financial performance in the hospitality industry. The metric, a function of both room rates and occupancy, is one of the most important gauges of health among hotel operators. The estimated total rooms revenue is an important component of the overall revenue forecast because it is one of the most significant sources of profit for any lodging facility. Other categories of revenue include food service, beverage and telecommunications, and another heterogeneous category of other income in which smaller amounts of revenue from sources such as rental and vending machines is usually also forecasted *(Uniform System of Accounts for Hotels)*. Also revenue from reservations can include a substantial share of total revenue. Different approaches to project revenue are available, such as the build-up cover approach and the fixed and variable component approach (Rushmore, 2002).

## 5.5 Destination related factors

This chapter indicates a selection of factors representing the viability of a destination as one of potential investment opportunities. Some are oriented towards the destination's tourism performance or potential while others represent the destination's economic investment climate and other socio-political and legislative destination's characteristics.

### 5.5.1 Economic factors

The **level of economic growth** of a market is an influential factor in hotel investment decision-making. Simply put, markets can be described as developing, emerging or mature. Markets with signs of economic growth are generally considered better suited for hotel investing than are regions that are economically stagnant or in early development phase (Rushmore, 2002).

These emerging markets are countries or regions that are restructuring their economies and offer a wealth of opportunities in trade, technology transfers, and foreign direct. They are characterised as regional economic powerhouses with large populations, large resource bases and large markets and are transitional societies undertaking domestic economic and political reforms (Chuan Li, University of Iowa Center for International Finance and Development). Furthermore, as being the world's fastest growing economies they will become more significant buyers of goods and services. Tourism, being a service-oriented industry, together with the increase of business travel due to the economic expansion both create opportunities for the hotel investor. To date, emerging markets such as for example the BRIC[6] and CIVETS[7] countries offer many investment opportunities, including hotel investments.

The **economic features and trends from the market area** are indispensable knowledge for making sound hotel investment and development decisions. "A market area includes the immediate neighbourhood surrounding a lodging facility as well as the larger geographic territory within most of the lodging demand for which a hotel will compete is found. The market area defines the boundaries of lodging demand and includes most of the lodging facilities that would compete with the subject property" (Rushmore, 2002). Once these boundaries have been set, the appraisal can continue with an identification of future economic trends, the importance of this information cannot be overemphasised, according to

---

[6] Brazil, Russia, India & China
[7] Colombia, Indonesia, Vietnam, Egypt, Turkey & South Africa

Rushmore. Categories such as the types of businesses and industries in the area and the economic diversification of the area constitute economic elements that assist in determining the strength of lodging demand and the likelihood of success for a new facility in the lodging market. While this information is pertinent for hotel investments of all three segments (commercial, meeting & convention, and leisure), the economic characteristics and trends however are most relevant to the commercial segment. Understandably, this lucrative market segment is largely influenced by aforementioned features and trends related to business activity. Not only do types and sizes of major businesses and industries within a market area indicate the potential for commercial visitation, the economic diversification of the area also indicates the level of volatility of the economy and as such hotel room demand. Office space absorption, employment figures, new businesses established in the area and airport activity all assist in determining the economic profile and projecting the future of the market area. However most relevant to the commercial segments, economic features and trends of the market area also reflect on the meeting & convention segment, which demand is habitually paralleled with that of the commercial segment, and the leisure segment, since an increase of wealth generally makes tourism figures augment.

Data about **demographic economics** and **labour economics** of the market area are both important to hotel investment decision-making. For instance, with regard to demographic economics, population growth and the age distribution of the population are factors considered by investors. However the former is not a strong indicator of changes in commercial demand, it usually sets the floor for potential growth in commercial visitation. The latter meanwhile indicates the availability and future availability of active work force. Labour economics relate to that work force and include factors such as the availability of a professional labour force and the characteristics of that work force. Different populations namely have varying levels of service-oriented mentality, or of dedication to work and perform, these work force features are all noticed and thought over by hotel developers.

In order to achieve big returns on investment it is vital for investors to time the **real estate market cycle** (Pyhrr et Al., 1999). Unlike stock investments, for which there are many different timing techniques and which can change in a day, timing the cycle is unanimously considered the best strategy for investments in real estate and hotel real estate. For investors, visualising the cycle in its entirety is the easiest way to grasp its predictability. Hotel real estate cycles historically are eight to twelve years long (Rushmore, 2002), less than other real estate cycles which are twelve to fifteen years long (Pyhrr et Al., 1999). The most prudent time for hotel acquisition is not when the market is achieving strong occupancies and many new properties are under development, but rather when new construction has peaked and occupancies and average rates are improving.

## 5.5.2 Tourism-related factors

The following paragraphs describe some of the indicators that contribute to the tourism characteristics of a destination relevant for hotel development decision-making. However positive future estimates of demand growth can be considered as the main determinant in hotel investment decision-making the factor **demand for lodging in the market area** is examined separately due to findings that have demonstrated that it does not necessarily have to be a crucial factor. Hotel development can for instance occur only to meet a frequent client's wish to be able to sleep at his favourite hotel chain everywhere in the world. This finding is confirmed by the literature: "Franchise affiliation is a strong attraction for travellers, mainly because of frequent guest programs and national corporate room night contracts" (Rushmore, 2002). Disappointing frequent guests is evidently not favourable. Furthermore it might happen that demand figures project positive but that there is reluctance from the investor for some reason. Despite being not essential in hotel investment decision-making at all times, it most often is and therefore it can be justifiably regarded as one of the most important requirements for project commencement.

The Elements of the Law of Demand from Melvin and Boyes (2010) state that demand can be defined as: "(1) The quantity of a well defined good or service that (2) people are willing and able to buy (3) during a particular period of time. (4) Decreases and increases occur as the price of that good or service rises or falls, (5) given that all other factors remain constant." The key element of the first part of the phrase (1) is "well-defined". The purpose of that emphasis is to ensure that the relationship between price and quantity is examined for the same good. There is no reason to compare lodging demand for luxury hotels with lodging demand for budget accommodation. In some cases, when occupancy rates reach full capacity the demand for a certain class of hotel increases the supply and this is when customers have no other option than to overnight in a different class of hotel, whether being an upgrade or a degrade. For this reason the definition of Melvin and Boyes is not entirely applicable to lodging demand. Besides, part of the sentence (5) indicates that all factors need to be constant. With a vast amount of economic, demographic and political factors affecting the level of lodging demand, constancy is a difficult notion to measure. Increases or decreases in the level of safety, rapidly changing economies and types of businesses, the intensification or mitigation of visa policies and the price elasticity of demand are just a few examples of factors possibly affecting the lodging demand. Therefore it is indicated that the forecasting of tourism demand requires that assumptions regarding demographic and socio-economic environments are explicitly formulated (Kaynak and Macaulay, 1984). According to Rushmore et alia the careful analysis of demand for lodging in the market area is essential in determining the feasibility of a proposed development. The analysis mostly begins with an identification of the demand generators in the area. Once identified, the current amount of demand they create can be estimated and this data serves as the basis for projecting future demand. The demand generator build-up approach and the lodging activity build-up approach are two techniques to quantify current demand and as such to calibrate the risks borne. There is no need to entirely

66

dissect both techniques yet it is important to emphasise both research techniques require much information such as information about competitive supply, seasonality patterns, visitation trends, potential lodging market segments and occupancy rates averages.

The *type of demand generator(s)* from the subject market area also exerts influence on hotel investment decision-making. It is/are not only the principal attraction factor(s) for visitation, it/they also assists determining the *volatility of demand* of the market area. The level of uniqueness of the demand generator contributes to the assessment of the market area demand's volatility. Lodging demand in a destination that is blessed with a UNESCO World Heritage Site is understandably less volatile than demand for lodging in a Mediterranean beach-side resort destination for which competition is fierce and level of distinctiveness low. Also for other than leisure segment servicing destinations the volatility of demand is assessed. The volatility of demand is also subordinated to factors such as natural threats, unrest due to political instability, and others. *Seasonality* is another topic affecting hotel developments. A concentration of demand in particular periods of a year can seriously constrain the financial viability of a lodging facility and therefore it may dissuade hotel investors from investing in hotel developments in destinations with seasonality patterns.

After the determination of the market area a commonly subsequent step is to assess the *market niche availability,* i.e. the availability of a unique market position or a particular market for which a product may be suited. The

67

advantages of servicing a focused, targetable portion of a market is that the need for a product or service, which is not being addressed by competitive lodging supply, will lead this niche towards the new hotel product and potentially even create new demand. "Finding the appropriate market niche not only is an important consideration for a proposed hotel development but can be equally critical when it becomes necessary to reposition an existing property (Rushmore, 2002). After the identification of the market niche or target group to be serviced the type of hotel can be determined and the hotel investor can look for available sites or properties (see chapter 5.6) and determine if an acquisition or new development is desired.

"The **lodging supply** in a given market area is composed of every facility that caters to overnight visitors in that market area" (Rushmore, 2002). The collection of this data is not only important for assessing the competition, the identification of competitive facilities is also essential for the much used lodging activity build-up approach for estimating the future demand. All of the hotels and other lodging facilities that operate within one market area are competitive with each other to some degree albeit with varying levels. Lodging facilities that cater to different target groups or that are differently classed are less competitive than those of the same class targeting the same customers. To judge whether a lodging facility represents major, lesser, or negligible competition appraisers have to investigate location characteristics, accessibility and similarities with the proposed property in terms of facilities offered, amenities offered, quality, price, class and image. Major competition is sometimes also referred to as primary competition and occurs among lodging facilities that are similar to the subject property with respect to facilities offered, class and image. Secondary competition occurs with lodging facilities that have similar locational characteristics but share few of the other major features of the proposed property, particularly class and image. Both attract the same visitors but the latter only under special circumstances, for example when all primary competitors are at capacity. Some hotels in the market area offer negligible competition or no competition. Such hotels are that dissimilar to the subject property that any crossover in demand is very unlikely (Rushmore, 2002).

In order to be able to emerge a destination or market area requires a sufficient level of **accessibility** to facilitate the in- and outflow of travellers. Depending on the type of destination attention to the importance of a destination's accessibility in hotel investment decision-making varies. Appraisals for hotel developments in metropolitan areas understandably pay less attention to the accessibility of the destination than appraisals for hotel developments in rural, remote or economically less developed destinations, as the former are expected to be better connected with other cities, regions or countries. "In the context of transportation studies, accessibility refers to the ability of people to reach the destinations they must visit in order to meet their needs and desire to visit to satisfy their wants. The ability to reach these destinations is affected by many factors, including the transportation infrastructure, travel behavior preferences, patterns of land use and development, availability of mass transportation services, and traffic management policies" (University of Minnesota, 2010). As destinations have to be accessible in order to cater to the needs of travelers and visitors, it is important to consider accessibility in terms of accessibility to important tourist source markets. A good accessibility with a nearby city is of negligible importance if the city represents only an insignificant portion of the tourist supply source markets. A decent intercontinental accessibility with connections to source markets can therefore be of higher importance than a well-developed regional accessibility. Accessibility can be determined by the availability of airport facilities, highways and the proximity to waterways. Also trends indicating accessibility improvements, for instance the construction of new highways or the inauguration of new air routes, are factors considered by investors.

## 5.5.3 Socio-political factors

**Safety and security** conditions of a country carry the potential to heavily affect hotel investment decision-making. Negative travel advice dissuades travelers to travel to a certain destination and this effect on demand is often a significant threshold for hotel development. A destination can be considered not safe when there is a certain level of possibility as a traveler to be involved in a hazardous or perilous situation. This can relate to small criminality such as pick pocketing, but also the risk of kidnaps and terrorist attacks can heavily affect a destination's safety level. Social intolerance, racial discrimination and poverty are some of the underlying causes of insecurity for travelers. Also natural threats can harm a tourism destination's appeal. Reliable and up-to-date travel advice can be easily obtained from governmental websites[8].

Also **political instability** can heavily affect and constrain hotel developments. If developing countries want to adjust to the world of increasing globalization and develop economically they will anyhow sooner or later face pressures from within and from the industrialized economies to develop politically. That there is linearity between political stability and the willingness to invest is acknowledged by the following statement: "The increase in FDI to developing nations has coincided with a growth in the number of democracies in the developing world" (Hess, 2004). In his research Hess also agrees with other researchers that FDI is drawn to stability and that stability is no exclusivity for democracies. In other types of regimes such as autocratic and authoritarian nations stability can also be found (e.g. China, Venezuela, Italy, Egypt [1981-2010],...) and also these countries receive FDI.

## 5.5.4 Legislative factors: Barriers to entry

**Zoning policies** or zoning laws are considered as protective characteristics known as barriers to entry and are issued by local governments to regulate the size, type, structure, and use of land or buildings in designated areas. These laws divide the cities into district areas according to use such as for

---

[8] e.g.: websites of the Federal Ministry of Foreign Affairs of Belgium or the Foreign & Commonwealth Office of the UK.

instance single-family homes, commercial establishments, hotels, etc. The local zoning code includes restrictive covenants that apply to a neighbourhood or group of homes or similar proposed projects. These restrictions give a neighbourhood a more standardised appearance because they control some of the activities that take place within its boundaries. Restrictive covenants can however also be attached to a property. The property may be restricted to only the building of a lodging unit without facilities or a sight restriction to not plant trees to block a view may be imposed. There are many other restrictions referring to building height, building bulk, building setbacks, signage, curb cuts and architectural design (Rushmore, 2002). Apart from restricting the zoning codes also govern the development of new hotels and the expansion of existing properties by regulating the permitted use of a site, setting limits on density, and requiring essential amenities such as parking. However zoning policies apply more to hotel development in the form of new construction it also applies to property acquisitions when renovation or expansion is required or planned.

"While zoning codes control the use of real property, **permits and licenses** typically control business activities" (Rushmore, 2002). Permit and license approval processes can take up some time and considerably delay and constrain hotel developments. One license that is essential for most full-facility hotel operations is a license to serve alcohol. Liquor license allowances vary considerably from one jurisdiction to another and its availability is not always granted, certainly not in countries with restrictive alcohol consumption laws. "Other permits and licenses typically required for a hotel operation include health certificates, occupancy permits, sign permits, food service licenses, fire safety permits and business licenses" (Rushmore, 2002).

Depending on the policies of the destination, property taxes levied can be based on the value of the real property alone; the real estate tax, or it can be based on the value of the personal property in its entirety; the personal property tax (Rushmore, 2002). Because property taxes can comprise of sometimes as much as 8 percent of a lodging facility's total revenue, real estate investors are not insensitive to any change in **tax policies** or tax incentives. Due to the impact on the financial aspect of the proposed project, hotel owners and operators monitor their property tax assessments (based on real estate value) to make sure that their property tax burden is kept to a minimum (Shah & Slemrod, 1990).

"Although zoning codes, permits, licenses and tax policies generally appear restrictive, they can often create value by limiting competition, improving the neighbourhood environment, protecting the health and safety of the guest, and regulating operational quality" (Rushmore, 2002). From a business operations point of view the limiting of competition due to existing barriers can therefore be regarded as an opportunity rather than a threshold. If there are no barriers to entry competition can enter the market quickly and the unique market position can evaporate quickly.

## 5.6 Site and property appraisal

The planning stage of a hotel development incontrovertibly consists of a site and property appraisal. Herein is assessed what the conditions are of the site where to construct or the property to acquire. A distinction has sometimes been made between hotel developments that involve new construction and hotel developments that involve property acquisitions, as some apply to both but some only apply to one.

In order to attract hotel developments the destination needs to have or make available suitable land or possess acquisition opportunities. Without the availability of developable land or acquisition opportunities hotel development simply cannot occur. Profoundly related to the zoning policies (chapter 5.5.4) the word availability in this paragraph indicates their difference and puts emphasis on the quantity of options rather than on the restrictive character of the zoning policies.

"Analyzing the site of a proposed or existing facility is the first step in the fieldwork phase of a market study and appraisal. The purpose of a site analysis is to determine the suitability of the subject parcel for the development or continued use of a lodging facility" (Rushmore, 2002). One of the first considerations is the **suitability of the site**. The physical suitability analysis investigates the site's size, shape and topography and detects potential construction impediments. Inconvenient site conditions such as for instance rocky subsoil or retaining walls can significantly increase total development cost and reduce the economic feasibility of a project. Apart from indicating potential construction impediments the physical suitability analysis also investigates that the size and shape of the site meets the preferences of the hotel developer, for both new constructions as acquisitions.

Depending on the kind of guests the hotel is planning to attract and the mode of transportation generally used by the guests the level of importance of a hotel's accessibility and **visibility** fluctuates. "A highly visible location is one that a driver can readily see while travelling at the posted speed limit and that allows for a sufficient amount of reaction time so that the driver can exit easily" (Rushmore, 2002). It has to be stated that visibility is not always an important consideration. Visibility is for instance important for a highway-oriented hotel that caters to travellers passing through an area en route to another destination but less for eco-lodges in a wildlife resort that work exclusively with pre-bookings. For the latter a great deal of visibility is generally not required. The visibility of a hotel can be enhanced and supported by strategically placed signage.

The **accessibility** of a hotel refers to the quick and easy access to the hotel from the highway or for any other mode of transportation. "Access is greatly enhanced if the property is continuously visible while the driver is approaching it "(Rushmore, 2002). This statement can be confirmed exempli gratia however again it applies more to ho a highway-oriented hotel or an airport hotel than for a beach resort or boutique hotel. Accessibility also has to be regarded in terms of the location of the proposed property in relation to the demand generators. Proximity and a good accessibility between the hotel and the demand generator are considered imperative. A hotel that caters to the commercial segment requires good accessibility with the business district or industry areas while a hotel that caters to the leisure segment requires good and easy access to the beach or the ski slope.

Following the physical suitability analysis of the site the hotel developers' considerations shift to the **availability of utilities** of the proposed site or property. The availability of utilities such as electricity, water, sewage, telephone, internet, gas, oil and services such as waste collection are important considerations for proposed hotel developments, especially in remote areas. The cost of bringing a utility to the site can have a negative effect on the total cost of the proposed project. Availability of utilities is often made difficult by resource shortages or by the impossibility to connect to a utility system. In case of full capacity of for example a sewer system a municipality can impose a moratorium that prohibits any new connection until the capacity is enlarged. These moratoria may represent only brief interruptions or may extend the project development for many years.

In case of property acquisition a **valuation** of the property in which there is an interest is also an elementary component of an appraisal. A valuation establishes the value of the proposed property and determines whether the subject property is economically feasible. "A project is considered feasible when its economic value is greater than the cost that was incurred in its development. If the project's value upon completion is less than the cost of its development, then it is considered not feasible" (Rushmore, 2002). The valuation of the property is not only important for determining renovation costs and assessing their contribution to the total cost of the development but also for price negotiations and mortgage deeds. A combination of three approaches is commonly used according to Rushmore however elaboration on them is nothing more than an aberration of the research goal and therefore not presented. Elements that create and influence the value of a property include the age, condition, current facilities, current amenities, location and the renovation history of the property. In case of acquisition of a hotel and not of a property that has potential to be transformed into one, the history of previous performance also provides a reference for hotel development feasibility. For the latter it needs to be reiterated that past performance is not always a reliable predictor of future performance.

## 5.7 Conclusion

In summary, it is correct to argue that the factors affecting hotel development decisions are abundant and miscellaneous and an all-embracing conclusion is therefore redundant. Indications of levels of importance are deductable from what has been written hitherto yet the following chapter will affirm the deductions with numerical weight assessments.

# 6    The assessment of the decision-making factors

## 6.1 Introduction

In this chapter the decision-making factors are being allotted two relative weights in the decision-making process for hotel investment or hotel development. Obtaining internal information from the investors and developers concerned has proved to be an arduous task and therefore the results are based on the seized information that was acquirable from published case studies, feasibility studies, press releases, the little amount of completed and returned surveys, the interviews with experts and the hotel investment platform TourismRoi.

## 6.2 The assessment criteria

In order be able to create balanced conclusion the factors are assessed a numerical weight that represents the level of influence the factors wield in the decision-making processes of investors and developers. The numerical weights will then be defended by means of a diminutive summary of the findings. The following table indicates the numerical weights and the level of importance they represent.

| | |
|---|---|
| 1 | Little to no influence on hotel investment/ development decision-making |
| 2 | Carries the potential to influence hotel investment/ development decision-making |
| 3 | Carries the potential to heavily alter hotel investment/ development decision-making |
| 4 | High importance in hotel investment/ development decision-making |
| 5 | Elementary for hotel investment/ development decision-making |

Besides the argumentation of the importance and the allocation of a numerical weight the level of manageability by the destination will also be gauged. Not every influential factor in the decision-making processes of investors and developers comprises of elements that can be effortlessly or rapidly altered. With this allocation the results can be subdivided according to their usefulness for emerging destinations. The following table represents the created valuations that indicate the factors' level of manageability or alterability from destinations' perspectives. All assessments should evidently be regarded in terms of a contextualised environment. Please note that the previous valuations of the alterability are not only subsequent but are also defined by additional information.

| | |
|---|---|
| a | Not alterable/ manageable |
| b | Barely alterable/manageable – Circumstances or responsibilities beyond control |
| c | Indirectly alterable/ manageable |
| d | Alterable/ manageable (given contextualised environment) |

It must be admitted that the succinct explanatory notifications are still utterly general and that the assessments of the factors and criteria deserve more nuance than that they have been allotted in this research. The generalising commentaries however offer unambiguous assessments applicable to a high amount of types of hotel developments and investments.

## 6.3 The allotment of the numerical weights

### 6.3.1 Investors' and developers' strategic factors

#### 6.3.1.1 Portfolio diversification

**2a** The diversification of portfolios can influence hotel investment decision-making for indirect or passive investors, who invest in a variety of assets and properties to mitigate risk. For the 'active' hotel groups it also sometimes is an important influential factor since these companies seek to have a representation in all key markets and segments and as such develop and acquire accordingly. Despite being occasionally influential it is a factor that anyhow holds no elements that destinations can use to influence investors' decision-making.

#### 6.3.1.2 Regulatory influence

**1d** For developers, having a degree of regulatory influence in the subject destination might influence decision-making and ease the process of development; nonetheless it is no absolute persuasive factor. Improving relationships with potential investors is possible however when the opportunity on offer is inferior investors and developers will be anyhow hard to convince, despite efforts of networking or invigorating relationships with them.

### 6.3.1.3    Alignment with stakeholders

**3d** Developing investors that have interests aligned with those of other stakeholders of the development process will be more willing to proceed their venture. As a consequence interest relatedness may have a high influence on the development. Furthermore it is an aspect of hotel development decision-making that can be managed by authorities when there are conflicting interests among particular stakeholders. Be means of compensations or incentives stakeholders opposed to a particular development may become more tolerable and supportable towards the subject project.

### 6.3.1.4    Partnership agreements

**3a** Co-operation and partnerships with reputed hotel operators and/or franchisors may assure investors for having a professional exploitation of their lodging facility. In many cases the partners are being consulted and they even also have a stake in decision-making. Therefore, depending on the type of partner, these partnerships can be of such an importance that they can decide on whether or not a development will occur. Despite this likely high importance it is evidently unattainable for destinations to anyhow create partnerships between investors/developers and hotel exploiters.

### 6.3.1.5   Proximity to the home office

**1a** For those investors that are involved in hotel exploitation it is advantageous to be in a relative vicinity to the subject project development. Assessing it a relative weight for its level on hotel investment decision-making however it is seen that for only some of those particular investors (i.e. those involved in the exploitation) it is in some cases important. There are many examples of hotel management companies that are US based but operate hotels in the Middle-East or Asia for example. As a result it is a factor that is categorised as 'carrying potential to influence' with above all the least possible alterability by destinations imaginable.

## 6.3.2  Project's financial feasibility factors

### 6.3.2.1   Forecasted ROI

**5c** This factor is the apparent driving force for the lion's share of investors for the actions they commit. Irrespective of those hotels that are there for meeting the wish of clients to be able to overnight in their preferred hotel in every destination of significance the vast majority is developed for gaining beneficial return. Forecasting the return on investment is a vital part of this decision-making and this process is therefore also categorised as probably the most important decisive factor out of all. The analyses for obtaining these prognoses are highly technical and constitute out of many other factors and these factors are in some cases alterable. As such, it is possible for destinations to indirectly affect the outcomes of the calculations. This important factor is therefore categorised as being one on which can be touched upon, admittedly solely indirectly.

### 6.3.2.2 Forecasted development expenses

4c This factor, of importance only to those developing, carries the potential to seriously hamper a project when the expenses exceed the allowable. If these expenses are of such extent that they are a menace for the financial feasibility of the project, the development plans may be halted. However it is one of the most important considerations for investors, it is a factor that only in few cases is causal for development rejection and it has a low determinative character. Despite the latter the factor, if noticed it is an investment barrier, can be undone by destinations by for instance amends or financial aid. Given some contextualised features which have to be considered it can therefore be categorised as being a manageable factor.

### 6.3.2.3 Forecasted operational expenses

4c The operational expenses, evidently of most importance to those investors exploiting the lodging facility, are an indispensible factor for assessing project feasibility. If the estimations of the operational expenses exceed the tolerable it may impede the development. Only in few occasions however it causes rejection. When there are particular costs hindering hotel developments in a particular destination authorities may consider financial support. Those responsible for the destination's tourism growth can also fulfil an assisting role for potential investors in their quest for financial statements of comparable hotels that are required for the approaches to estimate the expenses. Because not all hotels are eager to share internal information, in an attempt to preserve their obtained position in the market area and to not support possible competition, destinations' authorities might oppose them by means of alterations in legislation.

### 6.3.2.4  Forecasted revenue

**5c** This factor is dictating the majority of hotel investment or development decisions taken. Regardless the kind of hotel structure high revenues creates contentment among all stakeholders involved in ownership and operation. A healthy performance not only signifies more revenue but also increases the value of the real estate and returns on investments for investors. As a result it is allowed to rate this factor highest in the pool of considerations, mainly for active investors yet also for the passive investors. However it seems it is a factor barely manageable by destinations there are some options to indirectly ascent hotels' revenue. The creation of new demand generators or a diversification of the economy are examples of those.

### 6.3.3  Destination related factors

#### 6.3.3.1  Level of economic growth

**4b** The success or failure of a project is strongly related to the health of the local economy (Baum & Mudambi, 1995). Developments take place in market areas that are emerging or mature for the reason that hotel developments in declining markets are usually bound to fail, bearing in mind some exceptions, such as when entering the market for servicing a particular niche market. Anyway, in any case the level of economic development is one of the primary considerations for hotel development decision-makers. Because of the complexity and multitude of factors affecting and creating destinations' levels of economic growth it is in most cases impossible to alter the situation easily on short-term notices.

#### 6.3.3.2  Economic features and trends of the market

**5c** Adding to the level of economic growth, the destinations' economic features and trends are of immense importance for hotel development decision-making. In an attempt to detect lucrative market areas with opportunities for hotel development the features and trends have a high indicative value. However being a factor barely manageable policy changes can improve the destinations' appeals, for example by renewing infrastructure or negotiating with airline carriers for new air routes. Destinations can also play a significant role in the provision of required information for investors and also in marketing their destination as a good investment opportunity by highlighting the positive features and trends.

### 6.3.3.3  Demographic economics and labour economics

**2d** In order to have successful hotel exploitation there needs to be an availability of skilled and trained labour force. When this availability is lacking it might constrain hotel developments in that particular market area. Training and proper education are methods to overcome this hindrance, therefore the manageability of this factor is rated such. The demographic factors population growth and age distribution of the population are not seen as influential factors and anyway hold no level of immediate changeability.

### 6.3.3.4  Real estate market cycle

**4a** For investors detecting the right momentum in the market cycle of hotel real estate in a particular destination is an important tool for achieving big returns on investments, therefore it evidently influences their decisions. There are understandably no methods for destinations to amend the organically grown cycles of real estate.

### 6.3.3.5  Lodging demand

**5c** The lodging demand in the market area is expectedly categorised as fundamental for hotel developments.       Demand volatility, seasonality, the type of demand generator and niche market availability are considerations affecting the demand and as such the investors' and developers' decision-taking. The creation of additional lodging demand can be done trough the creation of other demand generators, the diversification of the economy, niche market specialisation, product innovation, etcetera. The options described are strategies well-known by all those involved in destination management and as such are not ground-breaking but only serve as indicatives for the manageability of market areas' lodging demands. Destinations can also improve the data availability for the calculation of the demand generator build-up approach and the lodging activity build-up approach.

### 6.3.3.6   Competitive lodging supply

5b Unless the hotel development caters a new segment or serves the demand of a particular niche market the competition in the market area plays a primordial role. Not only to detect the level of saturation or the vacuums in the market but also to be a source of data for the financial feasibility study of the subject project. Competitors' performances need to be used as a benchmark for the so-called lodging activity build-up approach. Therefore it is argued that it is a determinant consideration for investors and developers. The destinations' power concerned this factor is limited to imposing barriers to entry and facilitating the process of information gathering for potential developers with their possible prospective competitors, this could be done for example by chambers of commerce.

87

### 6.3.3.7 Accessibility

**4d** As indicated in chapter 5.5.2 the importance of this factor as a consideration for hotel development varies depending on the type of destination. Nevertheless one may argue that it is a basic requirement for tourism growth for any kind of destination, therefore it may influence decisions drastically. If the destination's accessibility is of that nature that it blocks tourism growth, destinations should consider measures such as infrastructure development to allow lodging demand to grow. Also the accessibility within the market is important, as the ability of workers to reach jobs, and of employers to tap into a pool of eligible workers, has obvious implications for the economic health of a region.

### 6.3.3.8 Safety and security

**3b** Again this is a factor that deserves more nuance than the general assessment it can receive in this chapter, nevertheless the statement of Buhalis & Costa describes their influences on hotel investment decision-making adequately. Because the impacts of natural disasters on tourists' travel decisions have a shorter duration than those of human-created disasters (Buhalis & Costa, 2006) destinations inflicted with the latter are more likely to experience investment withdrawal. To add a sparkle of optimism one can say that it is exactly this type of threat that can be managed, both directly as indirectly. Depending on the type of human-created threat (e.g. terrorism, pick-pocketing, assaults...) and its severity destinations can take measures to subdue them, both repressive as preventive.

### 6.3.3.9   Political stability

**2b** In political instable countries the future attitude of the government cannot be guaranteed and the political instability can cause runs on the exchange rate. Those countries are also likely to face problems raising taxes and investing in roads, communication, etc. The more political instability there is the less attractive and more costly it becomes to invest in those particular countries. It doesn't mean there won't be any investments; it just means firms will require a higher return to compensate for the increased risk borne. In any case it is a factor deliberated by investors. As political (in)stability reigns most often on national levels the more regional or municipal planning authorities of tourism destinations have little to no power to amend those situations.

### 6.3.3.10   Zoning codes

**2d** For developers, only in few cases zoning policies negatively or positively affects hotel development decisions. Imposed zoning codes such as height limitations for instance are rarely a threshold. For the tourist destinations it is furthermore an important tool for developing the destination in the direction desired. The high impact of real estate on the streetscape and the general image add to the importance of opposing clear zoning codes by the destinations' authorized organizations. It is therefore a factor fully manageable.

### 6.3.3.11 Permit & license approval processes

**2d** The level of difficulty to obtain the permits in a particular destination indicates the level of influence this factor possesses on hotel development-making. If obtaining all required permits and licenses is cumbrous in a particular destination it may impede developments there. As a barrier to entry it is however often designed for keeping off investment, while if obtainment is uncomplicated it simplifies the process and might encourage investments.

### 6.3.3.12 Tax policies

**2d** Notwithstanding its impact on the accounts of the subject hotel the research has shown that this factor holds little influential power when it comes to decision-making. Unless particular taxes are absolutely unreasonable, developments will seldom be cancelled due to tax policies. In spite of its low weight it is a factor that is manageable, bearing the financial situation of the destination in mind. Within the developing world the sources of public support are namely more limited (Evans, McDonagh, & Moutino, 1991).

### 6.3.4 Site and property related factors

#### 6.3.4.1  Suitability of the site

**4d** Fundamental in the assessment of the opportunity is the suitability of the site. Screening sites belongs to the main aptitudes of the appraisers committing fieldwork as it is very determining for the project's feasibility and success. Location does is paramount. Moreover, land prices are a sizable portion of the cost of opening a new hotel (HVS, 2010). Depending on the type of destination authorities have varying levels on how to cope with this demand for good sites. Being an urban destination it is most often difficult to be able to offer an amount of sites while an emerging beach-side destination may have a spatial planning that is yet less established with consequently more suitable sites on offer.

#### 6.3.4.2  Visibility

**3d** However intrinsically related to the previous it is suggested that the assessment of the factor visibility should be considered differently and highly contextualised. Whereas for a hotel operating with reservations it is less important to be highly visible, for a hotel catering transient visitors it is of uttermost importance. Also the manageability of this factor needs to be contextualised, as a lot depends on the availability of the destination's suitable land.

## 3.4.2 Accessibility

**3d** As for visibility also the assessment of this factor requires some discern. Not always vital for all hotels yet for most of mid-range or up-market hotel developers it is not less than a requisite. It is argued by Rushmore that a hotel should be in 20 minutes travel time from the demand generators, whether on foot, by car or by any other of the most commonly used types of transportation vehicles in the destination. For hotels catering transient visitors this factor could even easily be rated 'elementary'. The level of manageability is bound to the same principal restriction than the one of the previous factor visibility.

### 6.3.4.4    Availability of utilities

**3d** Particularly for developments on new terrain or in new emerging destinations in developing countries the availability of utilities is primordial. For hotels and resorts, known as energy and water gluttons, these utilities are simply essential. Nevertheless they have not been assessed 'essential, as the assessments refer to the importance of the factor in decision-making. It is imperative to note this difference! Also the level of manageability is very much destination or project related. The provision of utilities in the centre of Barcelona is for authorities obviously less difficult than on Maldivian atolls or even Swiss Alps. Nevertheless destinations can support significantly when financially permissible.

### 6.3.4.5   Property valuation

For acquisitions the property valuation is a crucial step in projects' feasibility analyses. It is very much determining whether the hotel development will take place in that particular property. If results are negative the developer will look for other properties, consider to construct or withdraw plans. As properties tend be privately owned, destinations have no power to amend on this factor.

# 7 Conclusion

However the initial intention was to assess relative weight by means of the analytical hierarchy process the seized research results are most likely representing comparable outcomes. By depicting the factors and criteria assessed according to the two variables of importance and manageability in an array, one can create a clear overview of all assessments and detect those factors and criteria that need most attention and are best manageable. See appendix 2 (page 117) for a more conveniently readable magnification of the table.

**Figure 8:** Table of hotel investment decision-making factors' assessments

| | Little to no influence | Carries the potential to influence | Carries the potential to heavily alter | High importance | Elementary |
|---|---|---|---|---|---|
| **Not alterable/ manageable** | Proximity to the home office | Portfolio diversification | Partnership agreements | Real estate market cycle | --- |
| **Barely alterable/manageable** | --- | Political stability | Safety & security | Level of economic growth of the destination | Competitive lodging supply |
| **Indirectly alterable/ manageable** | --- | --- | --- | Forecasted development expenses  Forecasted operational expenses | Forecasted ROI  Forecasted revenue  Economic features and trends of the market  Lodging demand |
| **Alterable/ manageable** | Regulatory influence | Demographic economics & labour economics  Zoning codes  Permit & license approval processes  Tax policies | Alignment with stakeholders | Physical  Suitability of the site  Accessibility (of the destination)  Visibility (of the property)  Accessibility (of the property) | --- |

When taking a look at the synopsis of the assessments outlined in the table one can note that the outcomes are far from surprising. In the end we are all assuming correctly that money is the pre-eminent motive for accomplishing hotel developments. Every single decision taken by commercial investors and developers is infused by their mindset of earning money; this of course is commonsensical and obviously does not need an entire research. Yet the inclusion of the financial factors has been essential in order to persecute completeness and to not neglect the most important reason why hotel developments occur and occur in particular destinations.

The financial factors have moreover a peculiarity that distinct them from the other factors in that sense that they are a result of the combination of the destination-related factors. The same could be told about the other essential factors lodging demand and competitive lodging supply. It is a combination of the economic features and trends of the market area, the type of demand generators, the local safety and security levels, and many other factors that make create a demand by which lodging supply grows accordingly and upon which financial forecasts are based. Therefore recommendations to improve the 'essential' factors are touching upon many of the other factors.

In the lower row of the table one can find those factors of which the destination has an ability to amend the outcomes in case they are being assessed for hotel development appraisals. It should be iterated that these are not the only ones of which the destination has a possibility to alter them because also in the second and third row the factors are alterable. Those factors assessed as barely manageable are often encapsulated by circumstances that are beyond their control yet not entirely impossible while for the factors assessed as indirectly manageable there are possibilities to influence the assessments by means of circuitously alterations with other factors.

It is evidently advised for the destinations' planning authorities to put special attention towards those factors that really matter for investors, as a consequence they will have to reduce investors' risks and create the conditions in which hotel developments can thrive. In the following additional and final chapter some general and specific recommendations are being formulated in order to convert these faint and abject advices into more tangible strategies.

# 8   Recommendations

In all cases it comes down to the creation or expansion of demand generators, whether being an enterprise, an attraction park, a festival, a museum or even... a hotel. The type of demand generator depends obviously on the type of destination and what that concerns recommendation can only go as far as the advice to create sound destination management planning that allows destinations to delineate their own future, based on their own strengths, weaknesses, opportunities and threats. A coordinated effort from all stakeholders can help emerge a destination management planning that can improve the destination competitiveness, increase visitor satisfaction, increase repeated visitations, enhance the reputation and attract investments in tourism and the lodging industry.

As hotel investors are attracted to destinations that have a lodging demand higher than its lodging supply it is evident that the main challenge for destinations is to create additional demand, given the fact that their goal is to develop and grow of course. "Hotel markets that cater to a wide spectrum of lodging demand generally suffer fewer significant downturns than areas that are dependent on a small number of demand generators (Rushmore, 2002). An ideal hotel location caters therefore heavily to all three of the major market segments but as not all destinations are similar distinction should be made on whether it is a destination catering mainly leisure tourists, commercial travellers or meeting & convention travellers, or ideally all three of them, as that would lead to the most stable occupancy rates throughout the year. For attracting more travellers from the leisure segment it is required to create new demand generators or to find a niche market not being catered to. For attracting more of the other types of travellers a diversification of the economy or the attraction or development of new industries are highly recommended. Also the growth of an existing business can create additional demand. These methods are of course all subject to the destinations' contexts.

I would also like to touch upon the topic of latent demand. Latent demand is demand that potentially exists in a market but for some reason it is not accommodated by the current lodging supply (Rushmore, 2002). It includes the unaccommodated demand, which is made up of travellers that defer their stay or settle for less desirable accommodations because the facilities where they want to stay have no vacancies, and it includes induced demand, travellers that are attracted to amenities that were previously unsupplied, such as in case in of an opening of a new demand generator. Indicating the latent demand of a market area may therefore persuade the investors or developers. Instead of them looking for opportunities the opportunity has to be served.

When researching potential investment opportunities hotel developers also often find it advantageous to employ a broker or a property search firm. By dealing directly with the seller, the buyer can however avoid paying a fee to a broker or a search firm and thus decrease expenses (Rushmore, 2002). For bypassing these costly intermediaries the destinations will have to be displaying their hotel development opportunities themselves. Therefore it is advised for destinations with sites or properties on sale to make use of existing platforms where they can network with and find interested hotel investors directly. Examples of these platforms are the annually organised IHIFs (International Hotel Investment Forum) in Berlin and Macau, or when preferred working digitally one can exhibit its opportunities to hotel investors on the website TourismRoi.

With respect to the site analysis it is seen that precisely those factors hold a high level of manageability by the destinations. Since they are significant considerations for investors and developers too it is well advised to destinations to put a substantial share of attention exactly on those considered factors. To every extent possible destinations need to attempt to have appealing property available, and depending on the type of lodging facility to be attracted they have to attempt to provide in terms of desired levels of hotels' accessibility and visibility. Providing for the availability of utilities such as water, gas and electricity until the site or property is depending on the destination sometimes nothing less than a requirement, but in those destinations where this availability is less likely and where it is seen it comes down to be an investment threshold the destinations could make efforts of support, whether being logistical or financial. Destinations' planning authorities will of course have to self-examine their situation and investment appeal and in view of that determine and anticipate on the issues that are the investment restrainers.

Imposing barriers to entry is another means to attract hotel developments and investments. However it may seem inhibiting it is argued by Rushmore that the opposite is true. "Barriers to entry tend to favour existing hotels, which benefit directly from a stable supply of competitive rooms" (Rushmore, 2002). Destinations should therefore carefully manage these barriers to entry (zonings laws, permit requirements, tax laws...) in an attempt to create a healthy lodging industry without excessive proliferations yet in the same time sustaining the markets' penetrability.

Another recommendation forwarded to destinations is the suggestion to have a high level of transparency. The more easily available the required information is for investors and developers the more streamlined the process of investment planning can occur. Make known the types of new businesses moving into the area and other types of demand generators likely to be developed in the neighbourhood, promote master plans and sites of likely future development if there are, and make available the history of the market area's development and growth. Furthermore the destinations' planning authorities can play a significant role in the provision of required data for calculation of the many approaches for appraising the lodging demand within a market area and the forecasted expenses and revenue of a proposed project. "Reliable projections of demographic and economic data are the most useful sort of information on which to base predictions of future market demand" (Rushmore, 2002). These and other data (see appendix 3) are required for assessing feasibilities and the destination can play a chaperoning role by being supportive and transparent. Destinations can make the information obtainable by means of governmental agencies, chambers of commerce or various specialized publications.

The recommendations provided in this chapter may be knowledge already held by those of the established tourism destinations' planning authorities but may hold elements that are new to destinations that are on the verge of tourism development and expansion. Attracting hotel developments will in any case be benefited when the consults presented are borne in mind.

# Endnote

Emphasis is put on the author's apprehension once more that the decision of not relating the research to one particular variable (e.g. weighing the decision-making criteria with a focus on small and medium-sized hotel investments, or for hotel investments in a particular type of destination...) contains a consequence that the recommendations based on the research results might not be fully applicable to all types of destinations or for any type of hotel, or on whether or not the destination is in the explanatory or development phase of the tourism destination area life cycle of Butler. It was the purpose of the paper to pioneer with a research that is reasonably general but one that is academically defendable and allows recommending all those involved in destination management, despite the scope which is admittedly immense. Due to the multiplicity of variables in this research the tourism literature has the possibility to be enriched with many other studies based on this one yet with a focus on one of those many variables. These research results could be of great value and can help creating an even more efficient and conscious destination management and hotel investment attraction than what the terse recommendations of this general research already aimed to achieve.

# References

## Books

Baker, K. (2000). *Project evaluation and feasibility analysis for hospitality operations*. Melbourne: Hospitality Press

Buhalis, D., Costa, C. (2006). *Tourism management dynamics*. Amsterdam: Elsevier

Butler, R.W. (2006). *The tourism area life cicle vol. 1: applications and modifications*. Tonawanda, NY: Channel View Publications

Carn, N., Rabianski, J., Racster, R., Seldin, M. (1988). *Real estate market analysis: Techniques & applications*. Englewood Cliffs, NJ: Prentice-Hall, Inc.

Chi Wing, H., & Loo Lee S. (1992). *Studies on the property market*. Singapore: Singapore University Press

DeLisle, J.R., & Sa-Aadu, J. (1994). *Appraisal, market analysis, and public policy in real estate*. Norwell, MA: Kluwer Academic Publishers

Isaac, D., (1996). *Property development: appraisal and finance*. New York, NY: Palgrave

## Newspapers

Michielsen, S. (2010, November 20). Kunnen de CIVETS het wonder van de BRIC evenaren?. *De Tijd*, pp. 20-21

## Publications

*From online journals*


Ardichvili, A., Cardozo, R.., Ray, S. (2000). A theory of entrepreneurial opportunity identification and development. *Journal of Business Venturing*, 18. Retrieved from http://goliath.ecnext.com/coms2/gi_0198-128825/A-theory-of-entrepreneurial-opportunity.html

Ballotta, M., (2004). Factors, actions and policies to determine the investment attractiveness of a territorial system. *World Bank, WBI/PSD Investment Climate Seminar Series*. Retrieved from http://info.worldbank.org/etools/docs/library/49058/ballotta.pdf

Baum, T., & Mudambi, R. (1996). Attracting hotel investment: insights from principal-agent theory. *Journal of Hospitality & Tourism Research*. doi: 10.1177/109634809602000202

Daude. C., & Fratzscher. M. (2006). The pecking order of cross-border investment. *European Central Bank*. Retrieved from http://www.ecb.int/pub/pdf/scpwps/ecbwp590.pdf

Donahue, K.D., & Roger, J.L. (2010). Volatile trends and hotel performance. *HVS Global Hospitality Services*. Retrieved from http://www.hvs.com/article/4985/volatile-trends-and-hotel-performance/

Newell, G. & Seabrook, R. (2006). Factors influencing hotel investment decision making. *Journal of Property Investment & Finance, 24*. Retrieved from http://emeraldinsight.com/1463-578X.htm

Özer, B. (1996). An investment analysis model for small hospitality operations. *International Journal of Contemporary Hospitality Management,20-24*. Retrieved from http://www.emeraldinsight.com/journals.htm?articleid=867173&show=html

Pyhrr, S.A., Roulac S.E., Born, W.L. (1999). Real estate cycles and their strategic implications for investors and portfolio managers in the global economy. *Journal of Real Estate Research*. Retrieved from http://business.fullerton.edu/finance/journal/papers/pdf/past/vol18no1/v18p007.pdf

Sturzaker, D., & Middleton, K. (n.d.). Managing risk in cross-border investment. *Gadens Lawyers*. Retrieved from http:// www.iln.com/articles/pub_236.pdf

*Nonperiodical web documents*

Anastacio, B.K. (2008). *A comprehensive look into hotel operation(s) and management.* Retrieved from http://www.mcu.edu.tw/department/inter-college/college/Web/StudentAchievement/TR/Bou%20Internship%20Report%5B1%5D.pdf

Ashe, J.W. (2005) *Tourism investment as a tool for development and poverty reduction: the experience in Small Island Developing States (SIDS).* Retrieved from http://www.sidsnet.org/docshare/tourism/20051012163606_tourism-investment-and-sids_ashe.pdf

Ashworth, W. (n.d.) *5 types of REITs and how to invest in them.* Retrieved from http://www.investopedia.com/articles/mortgages-real-estate/10/real-estate-investment-trust-reit.asp

Bichon, P. (2009). *Europe: refinancing a hotel in today's restricted debt markets.* Retrieved from http://www.hvs.com/article/4307/europe-refinancing-a-hotel-in-todays-restricted-debt/

Beldona, S. (2010). *Hotel feasibility analysis.* Retrieved from www.hrimtraining.org/.../Hotel%20Feasibility%20Studies.ppt

Canteras, D. (2009). *Hotel investing in Brazil.* Retrieved from http://www.hvs.com/article/4283/hotel-investing-in-brazil/

Chen, L., & Brophy, M.E. (2009). *What you need to consider before buying a distresses property.* Retrieved from http://www.hvs.com/article/4109/what-you-need-to-consider-before-buying-a-distressed/

Frehse, J. (2007). *Private equity hotel investments.* Retrieved from www.emeraldinsight.com/journals.htm?articleid=1616991

Goetzman, W.N. (n.d.). *An introduction to investment theory.* Retrieved from http://viking.som.yale.edu/will/finman540/classnotes/notes.html

Graham, I. (2010) *Chosing a hotel operator: the suitability of the operator to the hotel and the business*. Retrieved from

http://www.hospitalitynet.org/news/4036905.search?query=hotel+operator

Hess, M. (2004). *Foreign direct investment and political stability: Why investors like democracy and stable autocratic states*. Retrieved from

http://www.allacademic.com//meta/p_mla_apa_research_citation/0/8/3/6/6/pages83662/p83662-1.php

Kaynak, E., Bloom, J., Leibold. M. (2010) *Using the Delphi technique to predict future tourism potential*. Retrieved from

http://www.emeraldinsight.com.proxy1.dom1.nhtv.nl/journals.htm?issn=0263-4503&volume=12&issue=7&articleid=854271&show=html

Lynn, M.C. (2011) *Three steps of effective asset management: assessment, implementation and measurement*. Retrieved from http://www.hvs.com/article/5082/three-steps-of-effective-asset-management-assessment/

McCausland, G. (2007). *How to become a property developer?*. Retrieved from
http://www.primelocation.com/guides/landlords-developers-and-investors/how-to-become-a-property-developer/

Mendell, J. (2009). *Building a case for the future: Determining if now is the right time to buy*. Retrieved from http://www.hvs.com/article/4083/building-a-case-for-the-future-determining-if-now-is-the/

Muenks, J.M. (2009). *Narrowing the finance gap*. Retrieved from
http://www.hvs.com/article/3814/narrowing-the-financing-gap/

Murphy, L. (2010). *Opportunities turning into transactions*. Retrieved from
http://lhonline.com/development/reits/buying_opportunity_0910/

Payne, K.D., (n.d.). *The American hospitality management company: Feasibility studies are really market studies*. Retrieved from http://www.hotel-online.com/Trends/Payne/Articles/Feasibility_Studies.htm

Prasad. E. S. Rajan. R. G., & Subramanian. A. (2007). *Foreign capital and economic growth*. Retrieved from http://www.petersoninstitute.org/publications/papers/subramanian0407.pdf

Reid-Kay, S., & Lau, D. (August, 2007). *Hotel REITs: challenges & opportunities.* Retrieved from
http://www.asialaw.com/Article/1970974/Search/Results/Hotel-REITs-Challenges-and-
Opportunities.html?Keywords=Special+purpose+vehicles

Rice, A.W. (1999). *Institutional vs. individual investors.* Retrieved from
http://news.cnet.com/Institutional-vs.-individual-investors/2010-1071_3-281266.html

Richard, S., & Bacon, P. (2011). *Resorts: a focus on value.* Retrieved from
http://www.hvs.com/Library/Articles/

Sharkey, G. (June, 2008). *Hotel industry returns to owner-operator model.* Retrieved from
http://www.caterersearch.com/Articles/2008/07/28/321501/hotel-industry-returns-to-owner-
operator-model.htm

Shellenberger. D. (May, 2006). *Market feasibility study: Proposed hotel/ convention facility:
Lancaster PA.* Retrieved from http://newslanc.com/pkffeasibility.pdf

Sivitanides, P.S. (n.d.) *The real estate cycle and its double positive impact on property values.*
Retrieved from http://www.property-investing.org/real-estate-cycle.html

Thadani, M., Wij, I. (2009). *Hotels in India: trends and opportunities 2009).* Retrieved from
http://www.hvs.com/article/4195/hotels-in-india-trends-and-opportunities-2009/

Trick, M.A. (1996). *Analytical hierarchy process.* Retrieved from
http://mat.gsia.cmu.edu/classes/mstc/multiple/node4.html

Vasques, C. (2010). *The obstacle to make new hotels feasible.* Retrieved from
http://www.hvs.com/article/4684/the-obstacles-to-making-new-hotels-feasible/

Wickford, H. (n.d.) *Types of hotel ownership.* Retrieved from
http://www.ehow.com/about_5598328_types-hotel-ownership.html

*Nonperiodical web documents (without author)*


*Hotel Investment Opportunity Decision Model in Thailand.* (April 16, 2009). Retrieved from http://www.articlesbase.com/investing-articles/hotel-investment-opportunity-decision-model-in-thailand-869242.html


*A national framework for best practice destination management planning.* (2007). Retrieved from http://www.ret.gov.au/tourism/Documents/Tourism%20Industry%20Development/Best_Practice _Destination_Management_Planning_Framework.pdf

Jones Lang Lasalle. (2010). *Evolving structures in US hotel ownership: changing ownership structures.* Retrieved from http://www.hospitalitynet.org/news/4014155.search?query=hotel+ownership+structure

Hospitality Advisors Consulting Group. (2002). *Feasibility study of proposed conference center facility/ mixed use project at Civic Center Site: Troy, Michigan.* Retrieved from http://www.troymi.gov/ballot/studies/Feasibility%20Study.pdf

Hotstats. (2011). *UK Chain Hotels market review January 2011.* Retrieved from http://www.hospitalitynet.org/file/152004514.pdf

The Investor Insights. (2010). *Equity investors vs. debt investors: What's the difference?.* Retrieved from http://theinvestorinsights.com/equity-investors-vs-debt-investors-what%E2%80%99s-the-difference/

Terra Resort Group. (2010). *Terra Resort Group and MetWest Ventures form new hospitality company MetWest Terra Hospitality: Innovative Partnership combines financial expertise and access to investment capital with experienced hotel management team.* Retrieved from http://www.hotel-online.com/News/PR2010_3rd/Sep10_TerraMetWest.html

## Corporate websites


Alpine. (2010). *Risk management.* Retrieved from http://www.alpinefunds.com/default.asp?P=442559&S=442567

Azimut Hotels. (2010). *Hotel management.* Retrieved from
http://www.azimuthotels.ru/en/about/management/

Bank of America Merrill Lynch (2010). *Real estate banking.* Retrieved from
http://corp.bankofamerica.com/public/public.portal?_pd_page_label=products/industries/realest
ate/invbanking

Best Western. (2010). *Hotel development: Why Best Western?.* Retrieved from
http://www.bestwesterndevelopers.com/membership/index.html

BNP Paribas. (2010). *Real estate.* Retrieved from http://bank.bnpparibas.com/en/pid823/real-
estate.html

Cohen financial. (2010). *Services.* Retrieved from
http://www.cohenfinancial.com/content.cfm/services

Collier International. (2010). *Overview of Collier's hotel investment services.* Retrieved from
http://www.colliersmn.com/prod/cclod.nsf/city/98EBC45A25606686852574D4000BFAD3

Commercial Property Investment Agency. (2010). *Services: what we do.* Retrieved from
http://www.commercialpropertyinvestmentagency.com/index-2.php

Concept Hospitality. (2010) *Management.* Retrieved from
http://www.concepthospitality.com/consultant/management.htm

Crystal Hotels. (2010). *Crystal hotel management: at the heart of investment potential.* Retrieved
from http://www.crystalhotels.co.uk/management-brochure.pdf

Euroleisure. (2011). *Onze diensten: Ontwikkeling van hotels, resorts & spa.* Retrieved from
http://www.euroleisure.com/nl/onze_diensten/ontwikkeling_hotels_resorts_spa.php

Greenhill. (2010). *Real estate, gaming & lodging.* Retrieved from
http://www.greenhill.com/index.php?option=com_content&task=view&id=64&Itemid=157

Horwath HTL. (2010). *Publicaties.* Retrieved from
http://www.horwathhtl.nl/nederlands/nederlandsHTL/Publications/Articles/

Hospitality Industry. (2010). *Hotels: Hotel for sale.* Retrieved from http://www.hospitality-
industry.com/index.php/hotels/

Hotel Consulting International. (2010). *Services, consulting, Appraising, Analysis, and Research.*
Retrieved from
http://www.s191438859.onlinehome.us/HCI/services_consulting_appraising_analysis_research.ph
p

Hotel Investment Services. (2010). *Services.* Retrieved from
http://www.hotelinvestor.com/services.php

Hotel Solutions Partnership. (2010). *Introducing the Hotel Solutions Partnership consultancy.*
Retrieved from http://www.hotelsolutionspartnership.com/

Hyatt Development. (2010). *Press releases.* Retrieved from
http://hyattpressroom.com/content/hyatt/en/news_releaseso.html?Title=&Advanced=true&startI
ndex=1&FromDaySel=1&FromMonthSel=1&FromYearSel=1990&ToDaySel=12&ToMonthSel=12&ToY
earSel=2011&Topic=-1

International Hotel Investment Forum. (2010). *IHIF: giving you the competitive edge to expand
globally.* Retrieved from http://www.berlinconference.com/

Jones Lang Lasalle. (2010). *Hotel investment outlook 2010*. Retrieved from
http://www.joneslanglasallehotels.com/hotels/EN-GB/Pages/ResearchInvestOutlook.aspx

John B Levy & Company. (2010). *Structured financing*. Retrieved from
http://www.jblevyco.com/structured-financing.html

KBC asset management. (2010). *Asset management: analyse en strategie*. Retrieved from
https://www.kbcam.be/IPA/D9e01/~N/~KBCAM/~BZL1WYS/-BZL3T9B/BZL1W9X/BZL1WKG

Keefe, Bruyette & Woods. (2010). *Real estate investment banking*. Retrieved from
http://www.kbw.com/inv_banking/real_estate.html

Keybank. (2010). *Real estate investment banking*. Retrieved from https://www.key.com/html/real-
estate-investment-banking.html

Kingdom Hotel Investments. (2010). *Strategy: acquisitions, developments, asset management,
financing*. Retrieved from http://www.kingdomhotels.com/strategy.html

MHI Hospitality Corporation. (2010). *News and releases*. Retrieved from
http://www.mhihospitality.com/ir-news-market-data.aspx

Ontario. (2010). *Investment attraction*. Retrieved from
http://www.reddi.gov.on.ca/strategies_investmentattraction.htm

Park Plaza Hotels. (2010). *Development: new openings*. Retrieved from
http://www.parkplazahotels.net/default.asp?section=1159&page=5615

PKF Accountants & Business Advisors. (2010). *Hotel consultancy*. Retrieved from
http://www.pkf.co.uk/hotelcons

RLJ Hotels. (2010). *Development: overview.* Retrieved from
http://www.rljhotels.com/background2.htm


Starwood Hotels & Resorts. (2010). *Global hotel developments: development opportunities.*
Retrieved from http://development.starwoodhotels.com/development_opportunities/


Sree Hotels. (2010). *Hotel development.* Retrieved from http://www.sree.com/development.aspx


Sunstone Hotel Investors. (2010). *About Sunstone.* Retrieved from
http://www.sunstonehotels.com/overview/about_sunstone.cfm


STR Global. (2010). *Developers.* Retrieved from
http://www.strglobal.com/Products/Persona_Detail.aspx?personaId=8


The Highland Group. (2010) *Market & feasibility studies.* Retrieved from http://www.highland-group.net/marketstudies.html


The Hotel Investment Company. (2010). *Portfolio of investments: hotel investments.* Retrieved from
http://www.thehotelinvestmentcompany.com/hotel-investment-opportunities/hotel-investment-uk-portfolio.html


TourismRoi. (2010). *Investment opportunities. Retrieved from*
http://www.tourismroi.com/OpportunityInvest.aspx?id=58


Trinity Hotel Investors L.L.C. (2010). *Our investments.* Retrieved from
http://www.trinityhotels.com/investments.html


USAA Real Estate Company. (2010). *Investment strategy.* Retrieved from
http://www.usrealco.com/privateEquityFunds/investmentStrategy.aspx

Urban Land Institute. (2010). *ULI Development case studies* Retrieved from
http://casestudies.uli.org/

World Tourism Organization. (2004). *Survey of destination management organizations.* Retrieved
from http: //www.ebusinessforum.gr

**E-books**

Lawson, F., (2004) *Hotels & Resorts: planning, design and refurbishment.* Retrieved from
http://books.google.be/books?hl=nl&lr=&id=TTmbB1oDeogC&oi=fnd&pg=PP9&dq=hotel+investm
ent&ots=dod6F9MB9F&sig=grFKFyymYSGmqIxPn5qUEwlpO_A#v=onepage&q=hotel%20investm
ent&f=false

Rushmore, S. (2002). *Hotel investments handbook.* Retrieved from
http://www.hotelnewsresource.com/article32015.html

**Online encyclopedias & dictionaries**

Commercial property. (n.d.). In Investopedia. Retrieved from
http://www.investopedia.com/terms/c/commercial-property.asp

Debt-equity swap. (n.d.). In Investopedia. Retrieved from
http://www.investopedia.com/ask/answers/06/debtequityswap.asp

Foreign direct investment. In Investopedia. Retrieved from
http://www.investopedia.com/terms/f/fdi.asp

Hassett, K.A., (n.d.) *Investment*. In Library of economics and liberty. Retrieved from
http://www.econlib.org/library/Enc/Investment.html

Institutional investor. (n.d.). In Investopedia. Retrieved from
http://www.investopedia.com/terms/i/institutionalinvestor.asp

Investment banking. (n.d.). In Investopedia. Retrieved from
http://www.investopedia.com/terms/i/investment-banking.asp

Investment company. (n.d.). In Investopedia. Retrieved from
http://www.investopedia.com/terms/i/investmentcompany.asp

Investment trust. (n.d.). In Investopedia. Retrieved from
http://www.investopedia.com/terms/u/uit.asp

Private equity. (n.d.). In Investopedia. Retrieved from
http://www.investopedia.com/articles/financial-careers/09/private-equity.asp

Real estate investment trust. (n.d.). In Investopedia. Retrieved from
http://www.investopedia.com/terms/r/reit.asp

Venture capital. (n.d.). In Investopedia. Retrieved from
http://www.investopedia.com/terms/v/venturecapital.asp

## Reports (from private organizations)

Ascensio. (2010). *Company report (2010)*. Brussels, Belgium

ING. (2008). *Hotel vastgoed: Vastgoed in eigendom, lust of last?*. Amsterdam, Nederland

Kingdom Hotel Investments. (2009). *Annual report and accounts (2009)*. Dubai, UAE

J.W. Marriott Dubai. (1994). *Consolidated hotel income statement (1994)*. Dubai, UAE

.

# Appendices

## Appendix 1: Hotel development time line

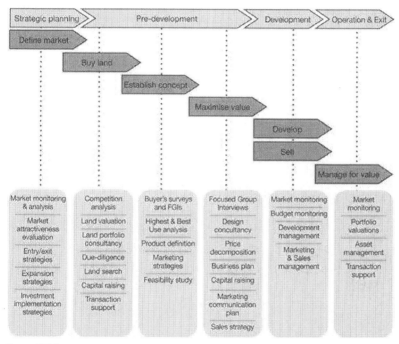

Source: REAS, 2010

The market area analyses and feasibility studies during which the factors are assessed fall within the ambit of the 'strategic planning' phase and the 'pre-development' phase of this hotel time line. After positive evaluation and calculation the process advances with the actual development of the property after which it will be in operation.

# Appendix 2: Table of hotel development decision-making factors' assessments

| | Little to no influence | Carries the potential to influence | Carries the potential to heavily alter | High importance | Elementary |
|---|---|---|---|---|---|
| Not alterable/ manageable | Proximity to the home office | Portfolio diversification | Partnership agreements | Real estate market cycle | --- |
| Barely alterable/manageable | --- | Political stability | Safety & security | Level of economic growth of the destination | Competitive lodging supply |
| Indirectly alterable/ manageable | --- | --- | --- | Forecasted development expenses  Forecasted operational expenses | Forecasted ROI  Forecasted revenue  Economic features and trends of the market  Lodging demand |
| Alterable/ manageable | Regulatory influence | Demographic economics & labour economics Zoning codes Permit & license approval processes Tax policies | Alignment with stakeholders | Physical Suitability of the site Accessibility (of the destination) Visibility (of the property) Accessibility (of the property) | --- |

*3.4.2.1  Appendix 3: Data used for determining changes in demand*

**Data used for determining changes in demand**

| Commercial | Meeting and Convention | Leisure |
|---|---|---|
| Total employment by sector | Convention center patronage | Tourist visitation |
| Office space absorption | Total employment by sector | Highway traffic counts |
| Office vacancy rates | Airport enplanements | Visitor counts at attractions |
| Office space being developed | Air cargo data | Total employment by sector |
| Inventory of office space | Tourist visitation | Restaurant activity index (RAI) |
| Inventory of retail space | Retail sales | Restaurant growth index (RGI) |
| Inventory of retail space | Visitor counts at attractions | |
| Inventory of industrial space | Office space absorption | |
| New businesses entering area | Office vacancy rates | |
| Highway traffic counts | Office space being developed | |
| Airport enplanements | Inventory of office space | |
| Air cargo data | Inventory of retail space | |
| Commercial building permits | Inventory of industrial space | |
| Housing starts | New businesses entering area | |
| Assessed values | | |
| Population | | |
| Retail sales | | |
| Effective buying income | | |
| Personal income | | |

Source: Rushmore, 2002

This table exhibits the types of data that best reflect changes in the hotel
room-night demand. Changes in hotel demand generally depend on the type
of visitation so therefore is the analyses ussually performed for the individual
market segments *commercial, meeting and convention, and leisure.*

52735288R00077

Made in the USA
Lexington, KY
13 June 2016